PAID
40p

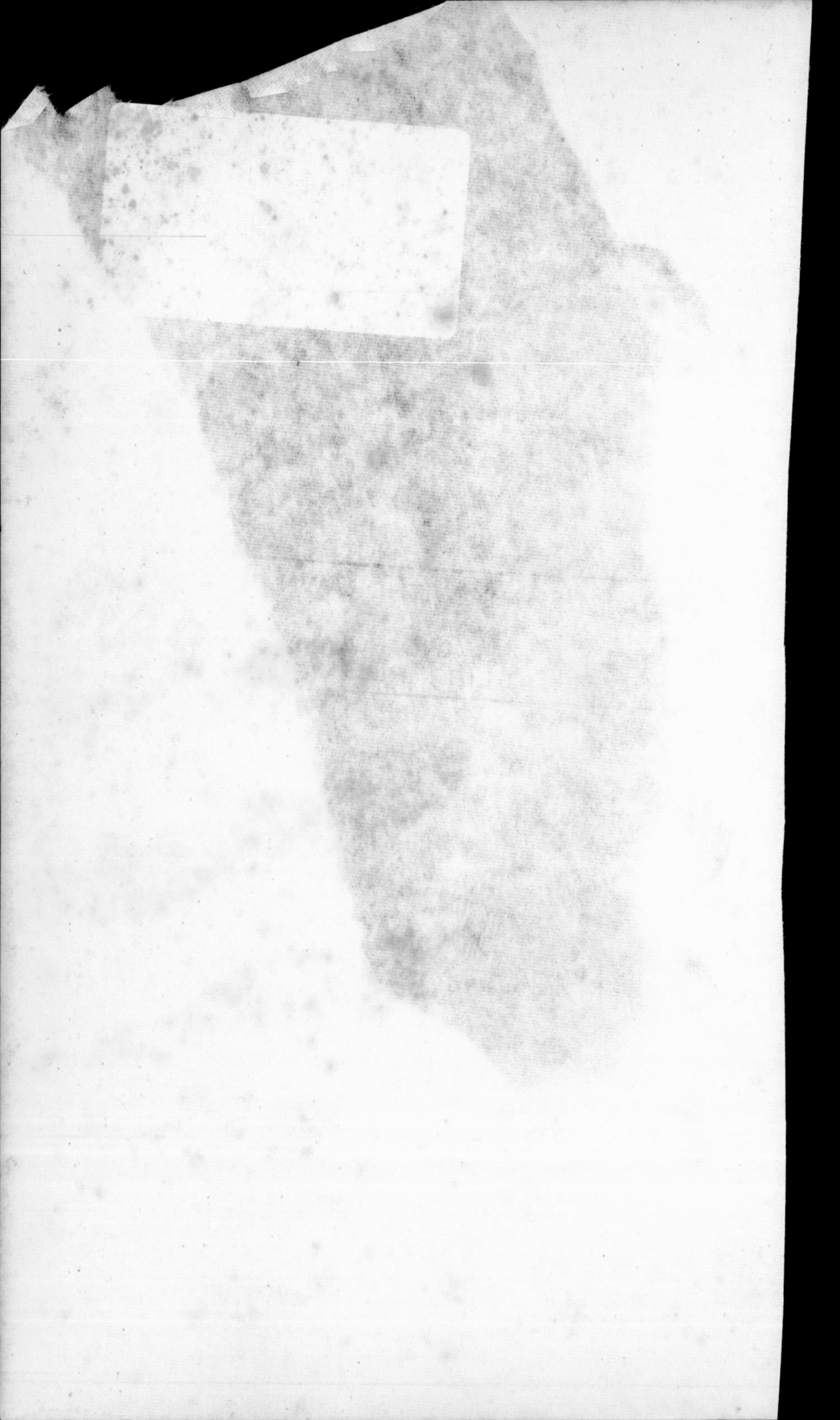

PRACTICAL BOAT HANDLING ON RIVERS AND CANALS

C. L. COLBORNE

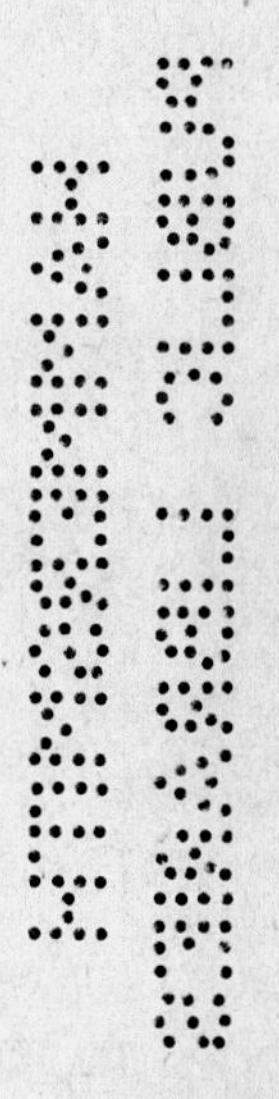

DAVID & CHARLES

NEWTON ABBOT LONDON

NORTH POMFRET (VT) VANCOUVER

ISBN 0 7153 7061 8

Set in 11 on 13pt Monotype Plantin
and printed in Great Britain
by Latimer Trend & Company Ltd Plymouth
for David & Charles (Publishers) Limited
Brunel House Newton Abbot Devon

Published in the United States of America
by David & Charles Inc
North Pomfret Vermont 05053 USA

Published in Canada
by Douglas David & Charles Limited
1875 Welch Street North Vancouver BC

CONTENTS

PREFACE

It is not easy to find an instructor in boat handling. There are expensive schools of sailing and coastal navigation, and most hire firms offer rudimentary tuition, but open courses on inland boat handling are rare. Yet, as pleasure boating expands year by year, complete beginners increase in proportion, and seasoned boaters seek new places to cruise. Often they do not realise how different are the demands of each area until they stray from their home waters. Visitors from the coast to the Thames often find the new discipline of locking most difficult, while river folk take locks in their stride but quake at the thought of braving the tideway for even the few miles to Brentford and the Grand Union Canal. Voyagers used to taking their time on the canals find the busy Thames locks frightening at first, yet the weekend Thames sailor, used to being shepherded through the big hydraulic locks by efficient if slightly brusque staff, may find the tiny locks on the Oxford Canal utterly baffling.

Most people enjoy reading about their chosen area in advance, and the David & Charles *Holiday Cruising* series caters well for this, covering each area in considerable detail. But such books can only spare limited space for advice on boat handling, and this companion to the series gives full instruction in basic techniques for the beginner. It examines in detail the differing requirements of various cruising areas: from the placid, uncluttered canals to the popular Norfolk Broads and Thames, and to commercial or tidal waterways like the Severn, Trent, Yorkshire Ouse and Lower Thames.

Although this book is as complete as possible, nobody knows

everything, and although I have been boating for over twenty years, many have been at it much longer, I am still learning things which I should have known years ago. I have tried to make the book simple and easily understood, explaining each aspect in a logical order from the beginner's point of view, not necessarily in order of importance. Nautical terms are kept to the minimum, and only information relevant to *inland* cruising is included. I hope that all who use the inland waterways will find it interesting and helpful.

To the Beginner

Please read the whole book at least once before going afloat, as you need a basic idea of many aspects in the art of boating while learning to handle the boat itself. Practise ropework in the garden and absorb as much theory as possible, so that when you finally board the boat, the battle is already three quarters won. Whatever the hire brochures may say about 'novices welcome', 'full instruction given' and 'simple controls', Saturday afternoon on the Broads or Thames is not the best time to learn boat handling.

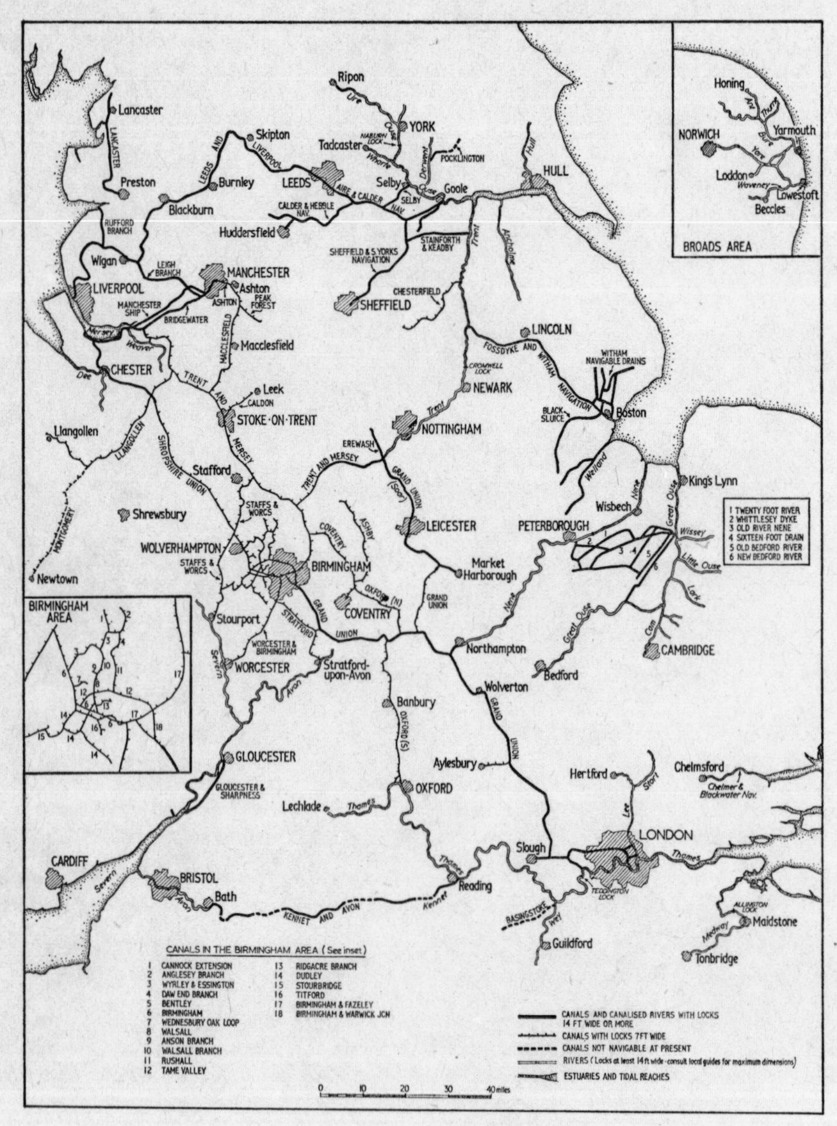

Map of British Waterways

CHAPTER ONE

THE VARIETY OF INLAND CRUISING

There are well over two thousand miles of navigable inland waterways in the British Isles, a great mileage when you consider how small these islands really are. All the major rivers are navigable, and most interconnect with the extensive system of artificial canals which went hand-in-hand with the Industrial Revolution, at first making bulk transport cheap and easy for the first time, then constantly trying to keep pace with the ever-increasing trade which they fostered. Some small waterways were improved and enlarged, while others had either insufficient money or an inadequate supply of water for this treatment. Some were financial disasters and should never have been built in the first place, and nearly all sooner or later lost their trade to the faster and more capacious new railways.

Almost every drop of water wide enough and deep enough to float a boat was used at one time or another for transport. Small rivers unsuited for boats were often used as a water supply for a parallel canal, for to do so was usually cheaper and more satisfactory than improving the river itself. The width and depth of a canal and its locks and bridges depended on the trade it was expected or adapted to cope with, on the supply of water available to fill it, and on the amount of money that could be raised by the public or private concerns which sponsored it.

Over the years, and for a variety of reasons, something like a thousand miles of waterway proved uneconomical or redundant and became disused, derelict, or even obliterated by railways, roads and other development. Recently, commercial carrying has virtually disappeared from small canals and river navigations; but now is the era of the pleasure boat, never dreamed of when long-lost canals were closing down. The waterways are firmly established as an important amenity, mainly state-run yet loved and looked after by most of their users, and never again will a single mile of waterway be closed without enormous opposition.

We are left, then, with a network of canals and rivers of various gauges, different characters and an infinite variety of scenery. From the bustle and efficiency of Goole docks and the Aire & Calder Navigation to the mountainous remoteness of the Llangollen Canal, from the green affluence of the middle Thames to the sooty squalor of the industrial Midlands, wind two thousand miles of the incredible achievements of a handful of visionaries and engineers and of thousands of 'navvies' (navigators) armed with little more than picks, shovels and horses. The waterways slice right through the middle of England and its history, and because they employ that most natural and sympathetic medium, water, they blend and belong in the countryside as neither romantic little railway branch lines nor (so far) new motorways have managed. Steel, tarmac and concrete are harsh and uncompromising.

So where on the waterways map would you like to start? If you have bought your own boat, you will probably choose somewhere near home to keep it, unless of course it is small enough to trail. But the majority hire a boat, at least for the first time, and the choice of starting point is between dozens of boatyards along all major rivers and canals. How to go about choosing your hire firm and the actual boat are dealt with in detail by Charles Hadfield and Michael Streat in *Holiday Cruising on Inland Waterways* (David & Charles), but a few words about the various cruising areas might be helpful to hirers and owners alike.

Three completely different types of cruising are to be found: on the Norfolk Broads and their interconnecting rivers; on the

Thames and to a lesser extent on other large rivers; and on canals in general.

THE BROADS

This area of Norfolk and Suffolk consists of a series of lakes, interconnected by rivers. It is the most popular cruising area in the country, and there are hundreds of craft for hire from many boatyards, some of which are famous as builders of craft you will meet anywhere on the waterways. For private craft, the Broads are remote unless you either live there or have a boat large enough to go by sea or small enough to trail, for unfortunately they are not connected with the rest of the waterways system.

The Broads constitute the oldest-established pleasure boating area in the country, and are a natural choice for the beginner because of their excellent amenities and services as well as their freedom from locks. They do, however, experience tides of a few feet, and although it is not essential to plan your cruise in detail in order to take advantage of the tidal flow, this certainly saves a lot of time if you are only there for a week. It is just possible to 'do' the Broads in a week, though this does not leave much time for exploring ashore, fishing, bathing and generally relaxing, which surely are part and parcel of a boating holiday.

At the height of the summer season, during the school holidays, the Broads can become pretty crowded, and the pubs and cafés even more so, but a boating holiday is a complete change from everyday life for most people, and the Broads, gently beautiful, are as good a starting point as any. Many people go there comparatively late in their boating life, having been on every other drop of navigable water in the country and perhaps on the Continent too, and very much regret not having done so before.

If you want to know more about the Broads, read *Holiday Cruising on the Broads and Fens* by Lewis Edwards (David & Charles).

RIVERS

Apart from the Broadland rivers, namely the Bure, Ant, Thurne, Yare and Waveney as well as some smaller streams, there are several rivers which form cruising areas in themselves. Still in the East are the Nene and Great Ouse with its tributaries, accessible from the canals via the Northampton arm of the Grand Union Canal. In the North East, you have the Yorkshire Ouse and some of its tributaries, and the Trent, which unite at the beginning of the Humber and can be reached from the West via the Leeds & Liverpool, Aire & Calder and Selby Canals, and from the South via the Trent & Mersey Canal. The Weaver in the North West is a beautiful and remote river, used commercially and with huge locks built alongside smaller ones.

In the West stretches the non-tidal part of the Severn, reached via the Staffs & Worcs Canal from the Midlands at Stourport, or the newly reopened Avon, and the Stratford Canal, also only recently restored, from the Midlands or the South East. These two rivers and the canals mentioned make quite a nice round trip. A glance at the map (page 8) will quickly reveal many other circular cruises, which are much more interesting than the there-and-back type.

Despite this, however, the most popular river of all is the Thames, in the South East. It has something of everything, winding lazily across the remote Gloucestershire countryside, a mere ditch of twenty feet wide; deeply incised into the wooded cliffs at Cliveden, ten times bigger, and swirling past the still busy wharves in the Pool of London on its muddy way to the bleak estuary and the sea. Of its many tributaries, only the Kennet at Reading and the Wey at Weybridge are navigable. The former will become quite busy when the Kennet & Avon Canal is finally restored throughout, but the little known Wey is rather more inspiring at present.

Further downstream, the River Lee and its own tributary the

Stort are also strictly speaking tributaries of the Thames, dropping gently in from rolling Hertfordshire, but they are more often explored from the Grand Union system with which the Lee connects via the Regent's Canal at Limehouse Basin or the Hertford Union Canal, before joining the Thames. And yet further east, the last of the popular rivers, the Medway, can only be reached from the Thames estuary, six miles wide, by sea-going cruisers, though there are several hire firms on the river. It is essentially rural, twisting through the unique Kentish landscape of hops, woods, oasthouses and the odd castle.

With the exception of the Medway, then, all these rivers are connected to the canal system, though because of the limited gauge of most of our Midland canals, none can be reached from the opposite end or side of the country by craft exceeding 6ft 10in beam. This factor must be borne in mind when choosing your boat!

Because rivers flow from high ground to, eventually, the sea they are equipped with locks to pass boats up and down from reach to reach. Locks take time to operate, though this is in many places the task of lock keepers. But rivers are also Nature's land drainage system, and this is responsible for the chief difference between rivers and the Broads, for cruising: their speed and level can change considerably as a result of rainfall somewhere in the catchment area (not necessarily where you are). This is not to suggest that most rivers are hazardous, except in winter floods—most are not, but they do demand certain boating techniques not essential on the Broads or canals.

CANALS

The canals and 'river navigations' (which are rivers so much improved for navigation and straightened as to resemble canals rather than natural waterways) are different again. There is often little or no flow, because most are not used to any extent for drainage purposes. Your progress is therefore little affected whichever direction you are travelling. Canals are usually narrow and shallow, some extremely so, which makes it impossible to go as fast as on wide open waters. They often climb or drop rapidly through large numbers of locks, which you usually operate yourself. Whereas rivers and lakes are invariably found only at the bottoms of valleys, canals more often run along hillside contours, through cuttings and over embankments and breathtaking aqueducts to cross rivers and deeper valleys, or dive into the odd tunnel through high ground. For sheer variety, there is nothing to equal 'the cut'.

The canals as pleasure waterways are still in comparative infancy. You can cruise on some routes all day and hardly see another boat, unlike older centres like the Broads and Thames, which are always busy in the season. Yet in recent years, great efforts have been made to improve the facilities on the canals, like refuse and water points and moorings near places of interest, so that you can enjoy the remoteness of much of the system without being so far from civilisation that the everyday requirements of life become difficult.

You may have a few questions or doubts about the conditions you will meet and your ability to deal with them and still enjoy the experience. For example, you may have heard tales of long queues at Thames locks, with boats waiting for hours to get through. This would be enough to put anybody off the Thames for life. But at most locks a queue longer than will fill the lock once is in fact unusual, though at certain notorious bottlenecks longer queues often form on a fine Sunday and can be relied upon on Bank Holidays. Except at weekends, queues anywhere are rare, and the worst locks are now being enlarged to handle traffic which was never dreamed of two hundred years ago when they were built.

The Thames Water Authority sees to it that unspoiled reaches remain so and are not flanked by permanently moored craft nose-to-tail on either side. There are sufficient places for overnight mooring, except sometimes in towns, and miles of river where you will only meet a few other craft during the week.

As far as the degree of expertise required in boat handling is concerned, most areas welcome complete novices, though each can present its own particular problems. On any busy waterway, you must for everybody's sake learn to keep straight and stop quickly. On the Thames you must learn how to put your boat alongside moorings and into locks on the engine without too much reliance on pulling it about with ropes. On the canals, and to a certain extent the Broads, this is less important as you are less likely to delay other traffic by either taking your time or making a mess of things. For the canals, you must learn how locks work, and use them properly so as not to waste water. The British Waterways instruction leaflet is very clear, but you will learn best from practice. After fifty or a hundred locks they become second nature.

As for all the other hundred and one things there are to be learnt, you can more or less choose your own standards, provided you obey the rules and cause no danger to others. You need not be forever worried about making a mistake, as it rarely causes more than a bit of a bump; but it is fun becoming as proficient as possible, and you will enjoy your boating the more for that.

Tideways

There are, however, areas where you *must* have not only a reasonable standard of proficiency in boat handling, but also a suitable and thoroughly reliable craft. This would apply if you are going anywhere that involves the use of a river tideway. No tideway is dangerous *because* it is a tideway, but everything happens on a much larger scale than the average inland boatman is really prepared for. Failure to observe the conditions and to react accordingly *can* be dangerous. The tide can run very fast, particularly at narrows, shallows, bridges and bends. Then there are commercial craft, requiring the deepest water, often punching against the tide and creating a wash many times larger than you will ever meet inland. Where the wind blows against the tidal flow, it can become quite rough.

None of this need worry you provided you know that you can handle your boat before you enter the tidal waters, and that it is suitable for the conditions. Nor does it mean that the moment you pass down through a tidal lock into a tideway you are taking your life in your hands. After skimming down the fairly swift Trent, wishing you could see over the high banks, and locking through the massive tidal Cromwell Lock with your heart in your mouth, it is something of an anticlimax to discover that the river below the lock is scarcely different from above. Between high and low tides, the difference in level is only a couple of feet. The tide takes about an hour to rise and eleven to run out, so the current on a falling tide is scarcely more than on the non-tidal river.

The tidal range increases imperceptibly as you travel downstream, and you have 52 miles to adapt to the changing conditions before reaching Trent Falls, where the Trent joins the Yorkshire Ouse to become the Humber. With a good ebb, that will take 4–5 hours, and you arrive at Trent Falls at around low water. Any ships have already gone, and you hang around either at anchor or beached on a sandbank wondering how the place came to be given such an inappropriate name, and waiting for the next tide to come up the Humber and speed you on your way up the Ouse towards Goole, Selby, York and Ripon.

No danger here. Anybody could do it. But if, while you are waiting there, a strong westerly wind should spring up, you would be sure to meet rough water up the Ouse, with the wind against the tide, unless you set off ahead of the tide and before the swell increased, wait at Goole for the first of the ships coming up from the Humber on the tide, and lock up into the docks with them for shelter. You cannot make the decision without some experience of how your boat behaves under such conditions, and of how to handle her for the safest and most comfortable passage.

While there is no desire to overstate matters, it can become uncomfortably rough even for the 150ft, 300 ton cargo boats, with waves breaking around the wheelhouse (which is at the stern). The other hazard is poor visibility. A quarter of a mile on the road is not too difficult to cope with, but on water nearly half a mile wide it is barely sufficient even for the seasoned commercial skippers who have spent their lives on these waters. Yet with the sun shining and little or no wind, and with the exhilaration of the unaccustomed speed over the ground, it will be a really pleasant and memorable trip.

Sandbanks can be a problem at low tide, but if you do happen to run aground, it is not the end of the world. Tideway shoals are nearly always of soft material, and at worst you may have to wait for a falling tide to turn and refloat you. The Severn below Gloucester is an exception here, so rocky and dangerous that in 1827 the Gloucester & Sharpness Canal was opened to bypass the bad section. Fortunately, the canal is still very much in use today.

Beyond the section of a river referred to as 'tideway', lies the estuary, where the water broadens and becomes salty, and the whole appearance is more reminiscent of the sea than of a river. Into these waters, strewn with shifting sandbanks which can give trouble at low water, busy with shipping and subject to sudden changes in weather and conditions, no one should venture without a basic knowledge of coastal navigation, a good compass, binoculars, echo sounder, radar reflector (so that ships can 'see' you in darkness or fog), and possibly a radio telephone and flares. An up-to-date chart is also pretty well essential—and of course a suitable sea-going boat. Size is not everything, and a 15ft round-bilge fishing boat is infinitely more suitable than a low hulled narrow boat of any length. The engine must be reliable and powerful enough to maintain a fair speed even against the tide.

Such areas would include the Humber, Mersey, Dee, Severn and Thames estuaries and the Wash. All of these are accessible by inland craft, and boaters may think, on consulting a map, that they can just hop around an estuary at will to reach another waterway, like the Ancholme or Hull Rivers, ten- and twenty-odd miles down the Humber from Trent Falls. Without the equipment mentioned and a lot of expertise, it is just not worth the risks.

Why bother even to go on a tideway? Well, apart from the experience of doing so, it is often the best way to reach a particular area by boat. As we have seen, the Trent meets the Ouse, and in so doing links the whole of the northern canal system with the South via the Grand Union Canal, with the West and Midlands via the Trent & Mersey Canal, or with Boston and Lincoln in the East via the Fossdyke and Witham Navigations. On the way you can visit the Chesterfield Canal, and if when you near Keadby you decide that the lower Trent is a bit 'hairy' for you, you can turn left and bypass it via the Stainforth & Keadby Canal; from which, if you wish, you can join the Ouse at Goole via the New Junction Canal and the Aire & Calder Navigation, or at Selby through the Selby Canal. Between Goole and Selby, the beautiful little River Derwent joins the Ouse; the Derwent is now being restored, and so is the little Pocklington Canal which leads off it. There is no other way to reach them. Above Selby, there is the River Wharfe, just about navigable to Tadcaster at high water, while the Ouse continues through Naburn lock to the splendid city of York and beyond towards Ripon.

From the western end of the Leeds & Liverpool, you can visit Liverpool, or turn south east for Manchester. The Manchester Ship Canal may be visited provided you arrange it in advance and have an anchor and heavy insurance cover. Otherwise take the Bridgewater Canal, roughly parallel to the Ship Canal until it turns south at the western end of the Trent & Mersey. Or from the Bridgewater you can now get to the Trent & Mersey on the more inland route, via the Rochdale, Ashton, Peak Forest and Macclesfield Canals.

A gentle round trip, which can easily be accomplished by a novice in a fortnight, is to go from Oxford, down the Thames to Brentford, which gives you several days to get used to the boat before the tideway is reached; then turn left into the Grand Union Canal, and follow it right up to Napton. Then turn left again down the Oxford Canal and return to Oxford. This can of course be done in either direction and starting from anywhere en route; but you must arrange to do the tidal bit between Teddington and Brentford with a favourable tide.

From the Thames, again leaving it at Brentford, you could take the 21-mile section of the Grand Union down into London, where you can gain access to the interesting rivers Lee and Stort. Or you can enter these direct from the Thames tideway at Limehouse.

From the Gloucester & Sharpness Canal, it is another eighteen miles or so down the Severn estuary to Avonmouth docks and the Bristol Avon. This is linked to the Thames at Reading by the Kennet & Avon Canal and although much of the K & A has been impassable for over twenty years, it is now gradually being restored as a through route.

Thus hundreds of miles of beautiful waterway are brought within reach if you use intervening tideways, which are as interesting in their own ways as any other stretches of waterway —in the design of their bridges, their commercial craft, their docks and warehouses and their surrounding countryside.

Having whetted your appetite for waterways, or at least aroused your curiosity, the remainder of this book is to help you to achieve a reasonable standard of competence. *What* you call a reasonable standard is up to you, but it is to be hoped that even those who will never stray more than a few miles from home will aim for the highest standards possible. Competent boat handling makes for safe and enjoyable waterways.

CHAPTER TWO

BASIC EQUIPMENT

The choice of a suitable craft, whether for hire or purchase, was covered in detail in *Holiday Cruising on Inland Waterways.* Suffice it to say that you should see as many as possible before making your choice. Go to your nearest waterway and talk to people on boats. They usually love showing off their craft, and most boat owners will readily tell you about any drawbacks they have discovered with their particular type of boat. Boatyards can be expected to emphasise the advantages of the craft they have to offer. There is an old argument about glassfibre versus timber or steel, but don't be fooled by promises of no maintenance required on a glassfibre boat. All boats require a certain amount of work if they are not to look shabby, and the older they become the more care they need.

If you propose to spend much time on the canals, you would be well advised to choose a steel-hulled narrow boat, which is built strongly to take bumps, scrapes and grounding which are all inevitable.

It is advisable to hire, rather than buy, the first time and many people do nothing else but hire. Boats are expensive, and there are advantages in spending say £200 on hiring a really well fitted-out boat worth perhaps over £12,000, rather than spending nearly a thousand on a 20ft, barely three berth boat with a little outboard motor, and the costs of licence, moorings, and insurance as substantial extras.

ESSENTIAL EQUIPMENT

Before you leave the mooring, whether in your own or a hired boat, make sure it has all the equipment necessary for safe and practical boating.

Mooring Lines

The number, length and size of lines required depends on the boat and where it is to be used, but however small the boat remember that a line smaller than 1in circumference can be fiddly and too light to throw any distance, and has a greater tendency to 'knit' itself than a heavier line. Lines of 1in are suitable for craft of average weight up to about 25ft, or 1¼in if the boat is particularly heavy for her size. For a boat of 25ft to about 40ft, lines of 1¼–1½in will do, but for larger or heavier craft, slightly heavier lines still are preferable. A look at fittings such as cleats and fairleads should give a clue as to the size of lines the builder considered necessary, and in any case a hired craft should have a full complement of suitable lines fitted. Make sure that the owner replaces any broken, frayed or knotted lines before you accept the boat, as these can be dangerous.

For inland use, the length of lines required does not vary much according to the size of the boat, as they all have to do the same job. All should be a minimum of about 30ft if they are to serve all purposes for which they are likely to be required. Craft of 35ft or over could usefully be equipped with 40ft lines, but longer ones often prove to be more of a nuisance than a benefit. However, keep aboard a couple of 70–80ft lines for unusual requirements like towing, pulling your boat off a shoal (shallow water), mooring on a tideway, or even making a temporary fence to keep cows away!

From the materials available today, the choice is really a personal one. Traditional fibres like sisal, cotton and hemp are in some ways the most pleasant to handle, but shrink when wet.

Artificial materials like nylon and polypropylene are available nowadays in many colours and qualities, and have the advantage of becoming neither sodden nor stiff when wet, nor do they rot. Some types become rather stiff when cold, and most have a greater tendency to fray than natural materials, as the fibres and strands do not settle together and grip one another in the same way. Have a look in a good chandlery to see the differences for yourself. The types at the cheaper end of the range, as with most things, are likely to be stiff, coarse and inferior to the dearer ones.

Lines come either laid in strands twisted together, or woven like sashcord. Should you be interested in splicing or similar ropework, the stranded type is essential. A woven line is likely to be a mixture of natural and artificial fibres, and is usually fine, pliable and pleasant to use.

The quantity of lines required depends very much on the shape and size of the boat, how many cleats there are, and whether you are prepared to change lines from one point to another as and when they are wanted. It is better, easier and safer to have them permanently attached, as far as possible. Lines are for tying up the boat, and it is the best means of doing so that indicates where they should be attached to it. In Fig 1, with only two lines from the centre line of the boat, it can see-saw in the wind and stream and chafe itself and its lines on the bank. If the same two lines were passed through fairleads or around cleats nearer the bank, this effect would be reduced. The boat in Fig 2 is fitted with main cleats and lines on both quarters (stern corners) and both sides forward (near the bows or front). The effect is the same, but the advantage is that the lines are permanently ready for immediate use on either side without fiddling, and can also be

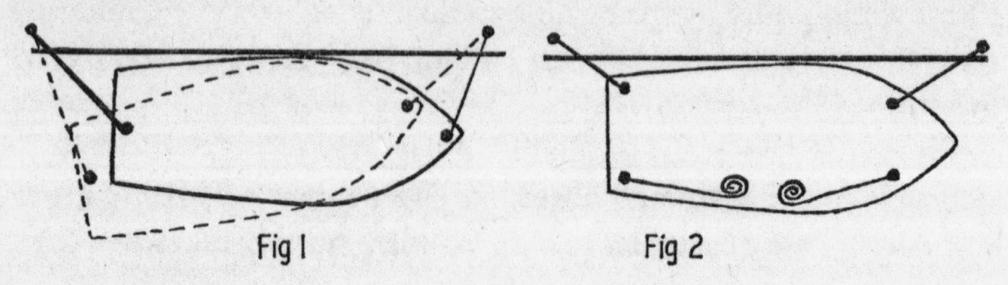
Fig 1 Fig 2

laid near the driving position so that someone can step ashore with both lines on reaching a mooring, to prevent one end of the boat from drifting away whilst tying up the other.

A line near the middle of the boat can be useful as a 'breast line' for a temporary mooring, or as a 'spring' to assist the other lines in keeping the boat in the required position when moored. Longer boats should have cleats along the sides every 8–10ft, though it is not necessary to have lines permanently attached to every one. A line each side at each end, and one each side amidships to be attached wherever required, would be a good arrangement.

Fenders

The purpose of a fender is to prevent damage to the hull by jetties, banks and other craft. They are hung over the side on short lines ('lanyards') where necessary, and most people like to use plenty, which is little trouble and can prevent expensive damage. These days, fenders are mainly of PVC or similar material, though it is still possible to make or buy rope or canvas covered ones. There are many shapes and sizes, but the smallest that will be of much use are the tubular-shaped ones not less than 4in in diameter. Fatter ones are needed on flared parts of the hull, so you can only decide what to buy after inspecting the shape of the boat.

Eyes or small cleats should be fitted at frequent intervals round the decks for suspension of fenders, separate from the cleats used for working lines where fender lanyards would take unnecessary space and get in the way. On boats with deck rails, the stanchions often provide ideal positions for fenders, but however many places there are, you are certain on occasions to need a fender at an exact spot where there is no convenient fitting, so choose at least some fenders with eyes at both ends, which can be suspended by two ropes where needed.

Lanyards long enough to adjust the fenders down to water level should be permanently spliced on. Always pull fenders up on deck when not in use, or they will make the smartest boat look scruffy. On canals with frequent locks, fenders are in constant use and must therefore remain down. Canal narrow boats, however, are robust enough not to need fenders, and since they fit narrow locks precisely could not enter them with fenders down. Some narrow-boat style cruisers are equipped with a few fenders for use in wide locks, and when moored alongside a hard quay (rather than a soft bank)—particularly if you want to prevent bumps and bangs disturbing your night's rest.

It is possible to buy shaped fenders to fit permanently on vulnerable points like the quarters and stem.

Anchor

This is essential for use on a flowing waterway in case of breakdown, and some authorities insist on an approved one (ie not an old brake drum or 56lb weight). The type and weight should be as advised by a boatyard as being suitable for the boat and the conditions in which she will be used. Preferences vary, but the Smith's Patent type shown in Fig 3 is the best general purpose type, as it is heavy and its points or 'flukes' will grip equally well in soft mud or gravel. The lighter but equally effective Danforth is one of several similar in appearance and efficacy. The CQR on the other hand, resembling a plough, is designed to dig itself into

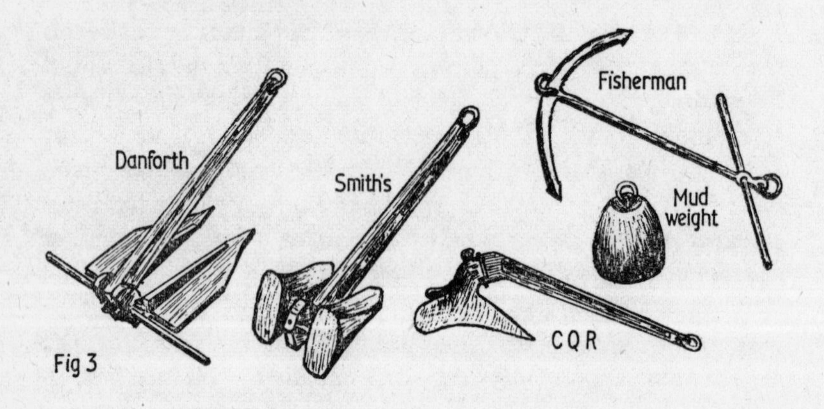

Fig 3

mud but is too light to dig well into gravel; and the third type, the 'fisherman' is designed expressly for gravel or shingle. The cross-bar at the top turns it so that the narrow points penetrate the bed, but in mud they tend to tear a groove rather than to grip.

Where the water is almost stationary and there is little wind, an anchor cannot grip the bottom as there is no permanent drag on it, so a mudweight of about 50lb is used instead, as on the Broads, but this is of little use on flowing water, where it will tend to drag. On a canal, moor to bank or wharf. In case of break-down, you can easily shaft yourself to the side.

Permanently attached to the anchor you need at least 10ft of fairly heavy chain to hold it down against the lifting tendency of the boat. The entire length of cable could well be of chain, but for all except the last 10ft mentioned strong rope will do, and must be long enough to allow at least three times the maximum depth in which it is to be used. Few non-tidal waterways exceed about 15ft, so here 50–60ft of rope will be sufficient. On a tiedway there can be as much as 50ft of water, so at least 150ft of rope will be necessary.

The anchor is mainly for emergency use, and must be kept ready at all times with its line or chain permanently attached and not borrowed for the washing!

Fire Extinguisher

A fire on a boat normally starts either in the engine compartment, in electrical wiring, or at a gas or oil appliance. Keep extinguishers handy near all of these, of the dry powder type which is suitable for all kinds of fire. (See fire drill, page 43.)

Bilge Pump

Timber boats often leak a little, particularly after storage, and any boat may take in water through propeller shaft bearings, water cooling systems, or as rainwater. A range of hand-, electric- or engine-driven pumps are available to dispose of this overboard.

(The engine should have an oil-proof drip tray so that spilt oil is not pumped, with the bilge water, into the waterway.)

Boathook

Of the three basic types illustrated in Fig 4, type a has a rough-cast galvanised head with sharp points designed to penetrate and grip wooden objects. If used carelessly, it can cause unnecessary damage to walls, lock gates and other people's boats. The head depicted in type c is galvanised or of brass, and is harmless when pushing-off but the second hook sometimes gets in the way whilst you are trying to hook something with the other. Type b, again with either a brass or a galvanised head, has rounded points and therefore is probably a more suitable choice. If your boat is large enough to accommodate them, it is not a bad idea to have both the first and the last types, as there are many occasions when a boathook must be relied upon not to slip. Select a boathook with a wooden handle, as those lightweight aluminium ones have a habit of bending double when used for fending-off a fast-approaching bank. About 6ft is a useful length.

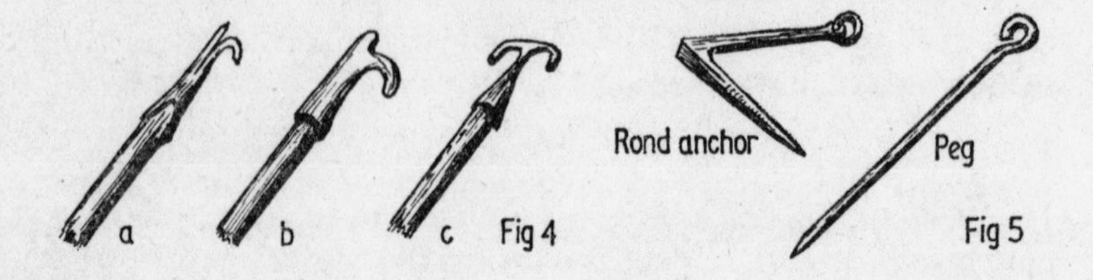

Fig 4

Fig 5

Mooring Pegs and Mallet

The best sites for overnight mooring are very often miles from anywhere, and far from being equipped with mooring posts or rings may not even have convenient trees. Carry a minimum of two mooring pegs, but three or four would be useful in some circumstances and would allow for losses incurred through leaving them behind or dropping them into the water. Almost anything will do for a mooring peg, such as a steel rod or piece of angle iron, but proper pegs made for the job are the most convenient, and two common types are show in Fig 5. The rond anchor is the safer, because it can be hammered right down to avoid tripping up passers-by and still be easily removed. In really soft soil or gravel, however, the straight spike about 18in or so in length can be driven in further. A wise skipper will carry two of each.

The mallet, of course, is for driving in the pegs. A wooden one is useless for steel pegs, and a four pound club hammer is better than a long handled sledgehammer. The latter is more difficult to aim and encourages bent pegs and bruised toes. It is also worth taking a strong magnet for recovery of pegs from the water!

Quant Pole or Shaft

This is relevant really only if you are in a long canal boat. It is used for pushing your boat off when you run aground or moor in weeds. 'Quanting' was the word used for the propulsion of unpowered barges by pushing on the bed of a canal, river or dock with a long shaft. Although a barge quant was often up to thirty feet long and weighed a good half hundredweight, yours should be stout but not too heavy and about 12–20ft long (if there is room on your boat to stow it).

Life Jackets

Make sure that every child and non-swimmer wears a life jacket while above decks or near the bank. There are many good designs on the market, some quite attractive, but life jackets are no good in their lockers, and there are too many avoidable drownings on our waterways each year. Most reputable hire firms supply on loan or hire as many as you require, which serves to emphasise the importance of this precaution. Some varieties can be worn either under or over outer clothing, but all must be fastened properly at all times. They are designed to float the wearer face-upwards, and if not fastened can turn him face-downwards or slip off altogether.

A few parents give in to children who complain about wearing a life jacket, or compromise by putting inflatable arm bands on them. These are fine for teaching swimming, but useless for saving the life of a non-swimmer, because unless the arms are held down they simply float off. Also, note the difference between a proper life jacket (which will float an unconscious person) and a buoyancy aid (which is what most of the lightweight jacket types really are). The latter are quite adequate for inland use, but for tideway or coastal work where help may be beyond swimming distance and unconsciousness could occur due to exposure or shock, inflatable or kapok life jackets must be worn by everybody, swimmer or not, who will be on deck, and must be available for the rest of the crew in case of capsizing or sinking.

Official statistics of drownings in the UK vary, but of some 3,000 people drowned in one recent year 100 died as a result of boating accidents around the coast. The Thames claimed 20–30, of whom only 5–10 were involved with boating. These figures, though sobering, should put the matter into perspective, especially when you consider that hundreds fall into the Thames alone, usually in the vicinity of locks and nearly always as a result of poor boat handling or poor ropework, and that over fifty per cent of all adults in the UK cannot swim.

Lifebelts

Carry at least one lifebelt, which is a ring of either cork or plastic like the fenders, for throwing to anybody who might fall overboard. Unless you are experienced in handling the boat, it could be some time before the victim is recovered. Tie the lifebelt, with about 60ft of light line neatly coiled, to the boat, using a quick-release hitch. You cannot throw it more than this distance, and it could save time to be able to haul it back to the boat, with the victim or for a second throw.

Boarding Ladder

Having kept your victim afloat and hauled him alongside, it is often virtually impossible to get him back aboard if he is exhausted, due to the height of the hull and the lack of footholds. On such craft, a simple hook-on ladder long enough to extend about 3ft under water is a wise extra. Larger boats can be fitted with a permanent ladder over the stern with a hinged lower section which can be raised clear of the water when not in use.

First-Aid Kit

Always carry a kit containing adhesive plasters, bandages, adhesive tape, burn dressings, cotton wool, antiseptic, antiseptic cream, lint, sal volatile and scissors. A booklet on elementary First-Aid or the leaflet supplied with the kit should also be to hand, as well as instructions for artificial resuscitation. This subject should be studied and memorised, as to apply it quickly enough may make the difference between life and death.

General Safety

Every piece of equipment—particularly safety equipment—must be kept accessible and in good condition, so that it can be relied upon when needed. Decks should be treated with non-slip material or paint and kept tidy to prevent tripping or slipping. Gas and paraffin appliances and the engine and its compartment must be kept clean to minimise fire risk, and wiring and gas pipes must be properly supported clear of hot exhaust pipes, etc, and moving or vibrating parts. Filler caps for paraffin, petrol, diesel and water, and sewage pump-out outlets, must be clearly and accurately marked to avoid filling with the wrong fluid.

Bottled gas is denser than air, so bottles must be housed above water level in compartments which drain overboard, to avoid gas accumulation in the boat which could cause asphyxia or explosion. Do not use gas or oil heaters without ventilation, as they can asphyxiate too, by burning all the available oxygen. Ban smoking below decks, particularly in bed. Do not take alcohol in any quantity before going or while on deck, as it impairs judgement and causes rapid loss of body heat should you fall into the water, which in turn can cause unconsciousness.

Most important of all: study the 'Fire' and 'Man Overboard' drills at the end of Chapter three before going afloat.

Licence

Before a boat may be used on most inland waterways, a licence must first be obtained from the navigation authority concerned. At the time of writing, most canals and some rivers are run by the British Waterways Board, but other rivers are administered by separate bodies, such as the regional water authorities in charge of their particular catchment and distribution areas. Guide books to each specific area should give all the information you need and the address to contact.

Most authorities license craft annually or for shorter periods in the case of visiting boats, and most also make a small charge for a tender. Note that a tender with an outboard motor, even if little more than a rubber tyre itself, immediately becomes a launch and is subject to the charges for that type of vessel.

OPTIONAL EXTRAS

Tender

If you keep your boat on a midstream mooring, a small boat will be necessary in order to reach her, called a tender because it is used to tend the parent vessel. It can also be used for exploring backwaters or derelict canals too shallow for the cruiser, or for the odd emergency like taking a line to the bank in order to pull the boat off a shoal.

A tender, for all its usefulness, spends most of its time getting in the way. It should preferably be small enough to lift and stow aboard your boat, either on deck or on davits over the stern. In the latter case, choose a tender which is short enough not to stick out beyond the sides of the cruiser, otherwise damage is almost inevitable when locking or mooring. If the cruiser is too small for this, you are better off without a tender, which when towed everywhere bumps into your boat every time you stop and makes a nuisance of itself generally.

For the smaller cruiser, an inflatable tender is probably the most popular choice, for even if it is more convenient to keep it inflated, it is both light and fairly stable. A very small glassfibre or foam-rubber dinghy is usually most unstable when afloat.

In *Holiday Cruising on Inland Waterways* there is much useful information about the fitting out and maintenance of boats, so it is not necessary to comment further here. However, you would be well advised to obtain a copy of the specifications laid down by the old Thames Conservancy for engine-, gas- and sanitary installations. Whether or not you intend to use the Thames, these amount to a comprehensive code on safety and anti-pollution measures which any waterways user should be only too ready to follow.

Over and above the items listed, most of which are essential for competent boating and safety, it is possible to fill your boat with gadgets and equipment for every conceivable purpose, some of it quite useful even on inland waterways! A glance at one of the yachting magazines or browsing around a chandlery will give an idea of the vast number of extras available. But do provide the essentials first, then please yourself about the gimmicks.

An item which cannot be described as either is an ensign. All British craft are entitled to fly the Red Ensign, which consists of a Union Jack in the top left corner of a red ground, usually from a staff at the stern. Strictly speaking, a boat is improperly dressed without it, although canal craft and small commercial craft usually do not bother; nor do most hire firms. The ensign is worn from sunrise to sunset, but only when the boat is in use (including temporary daytime stops). Other flags, such as a Union Jack, Blue or White Ensign, or a Red Ensign with any defacement, may not be worn except by certain authorised people, who know who they are. Craft under foreign command, like a boat hired by a foreign visitor, may wear the appropriate maritime flag of that country, and many foreign hirers bring their own with them. When cruising in foreign waters, it is a courtesy to fly the flag of the country you are in at the masthead as well as your own at the stern.

Toilets
Whilst not obligatory, all cabin cruisers should have a self-contained toilet which can be emptied at sanitary stations, or a sewage holding tank which can be pumped out ashore. Sea toilets which discharge into the waterway are seldom permitted.

Plate 1 (*above*) A boarding ladder, invaluable for recovering a 'man overboard', must reach well below the surface. This model is shown folded up when not in use, or could be removed completely;
Plates 2 and 3 (*below, left and right*) The correct way to coil a rope, whether in the hand or on deck, with neat, clockwise turns

Plate 4 (*above*) Helmsman's view from a Caribbean. The semicircular bows provide little indication of the boat's course. Forward-control cruisers can at first prove difficult to steer straight;
Plate 5 (*below*) A Caribbean cruiser sets off from John Bushnell's yard at Wargrave, Thames, early in the season

CHAPTER THREE

THE FIRST TRIP

Anyone who expects driving a boat to be anything like driving a car is in for a shock. The two are about as dissimilar as the techniques for playing the guitar and the piano. Both require practice and skill, though success at one is of limited assistance in mastering the other, and can be a disadvantage. Neither could be described as easier than the other—just different. Often, wives or children who do not drive, and therefore do not have too many preconceived ideas to distract them, will master boat-handling much more easily than Father. Some men find this difficult to swallow, but in many cases it would be much better to let the family take the boat whilst Dad sees to lines, locks and cups of tea.

How is it different?

For one thing, a car is normally held steady, whether moving or not, by friction with the road. It will only normally move when and how its driver tells it to. But a boat will float about in any direction it wishes, unless given clear instructions either to keep still or to travel in a particular direction. And even then it argues with you! Then there is the steering, which may or may not be operated by a car-type steering wheel. This turns a rudder which is situated at the stern, and it is therefore the back and not the front that swings when the wheel is turned, a phenomenon with which a few people never do come to terms. On the credit side, there are no gears or clutch to bother about once you are going.

The gears and throttle are frequently operated by a single lever which first engages forward or reverse gear and then increases the engine speed. Finally, there are no brakes either—you have to reverse the engine until the boat stops and then remember to put the lever to neutral.

Even with the benefit of an enlightened instructor for ten minutes, you will only learn a few rudimentary points, which is a far cry from being able to apply them. A beginner with great aptitude, having studied the theory in advance, can become proficient in all basic procedures in about a day. For most, it will take a little longer, particularly when several people are trying to learn on the same boat together, as frequently happens when a family or friends hire a boat and the time available for learning is limited. Just as you are becoming competent, your holiday is over, and you will have to re-learn most of it next year. Even with your own boat, to become expert can take years, and it is surprising how quickly you get out of touch.

STARTING OFF

Let us assume that you and a crew of two able-bodied companions are now aboard your boat, which is equipped with all necessary gear including steering by means of a wheel (helm), still tied up to a good bankside landing stage on a fairly quiet day. You have all studied this book beforehand, have turned on battery, fuel etc, and attended to routine maintenance like checking fuel and oil.

Start the engine and warm it up until it will idle without stalling.

Tell your crew to 'let go' (untie the mooring lines) and to come back aboard, pushing the boat out bodily sideways as they do so. If anything, the bows should be pushed a little harder to point slightly away from the bank and from other moored craft. It is possible to get away almost entirely on the engine, but there are more important things to master first. Now, having made sure that your wheel is amidships (with the rudder or outboard straight), engage forward gear. You are off.

The rule of the road, when passing other vessels, is to keep to the *right* (see Chapter nine).

Coiling a Rope

As soon as you are under way, make sure that your crew immediately coil all lines ready for their next use. Ropes dropped in a heap on deck, though a common sight, are untidy, often difficult to unravel when required, and liable to trip somebody up. There are only two satisfactory methods of coiling lines of the length you will be using for mooring, and with both you *start at the end that is fixed to the boat* (the standing end as it is correctly called).

To coil over the hand, lay the line in neat *clockwise* coils with the other hand, ensuring that each turn is a similar size and lies flat (see Plates two and three). Any turn that tries to twist itself into an 8-shape must be twisted in the opposite direction until it lies sweetly. Each twist must be free to run the whole uncoiled length of the rope and fall off the end, otherwise for each turn there will be a kink in the opposite direction, which must be shaken from the end of the line before the coil can be completed.

If a line is coiled from the running end, these kinks become trapped, and any attempt to remove them by pulling only results in unstranding and weakening the line. Repeated mis-coiling of a line in this way, and use of it in a kinked state, completely ruins it and will eventually cause it to break.

With a line too long or heavy to hold in the hand, coiling down on the deck will be more satisfactory. Again, start at the standing end, twisting the line as you pay it with both hands on to the coil.

STEERING

Your crew have sorted out the lines and taken in the fenders, and you are at the helm and probably steering rather crookedly, turning the wheel as in a car in the direction required. You will notice at once how slow the boat is to respond to the wheel, and most people instinctively try to correct this by oversteering. To turn a boat is quite easy, but keeping straight is much more difficult, especially at low speeds.

A boat behaves very differently from a car where, when you turn the wheel, it is the front that immediately swings sideways, followed by the back on a tighter radius. If you turn too soon, your rear wheels mount the kerb. With a boat, it is the stern that swings wide, in the opposite direction to the turn, and your chief concern is to avoid hitting something on the *outside* of the turn. (See Fig 6). This is a particular problem when leaving a mooring, where if the stern has not room to swing *towards* the bank, the bows cannot move *away* from it in the way that the front of a car moves away from the kerb.

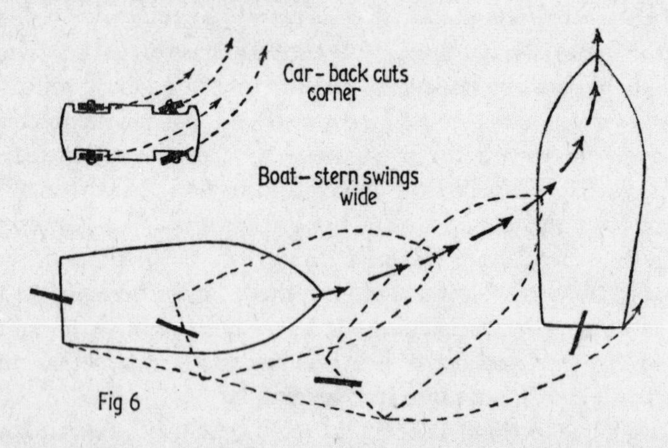

Fig 6

A boat spends its time trying to drift around at the whim of winds and currents, and will not automatically keep straight just because you keep the helm still. When the boat tends to wander away to one side, say the port or left side, gently correct this by steering slightly towards the other, that is starboard or right side. It will probably then swing away to starboard, which must also be corrected. Try to react in time to correct each swing before it really develops, and you will eventually be able to steer straight. The faster you are going, the easier it will normally be, for the hull will then keep itself fairly straight.

It is not always easy to tell that a boat *is* beginning to veer off course before the direction has altered quite considerably.

Sometimes the first indication is that one bank is closer than before. It is best to find a point of reference on your boat and line it up with distant scenery. The further aft the steering position, the better your view and the greater your chances of keeping straight. From the tiller of a 70ft narrow boat you can detect a variation of a fraction of a degree, while on the modern forward-control Broads cruisers there is often no point of reference ahead of you on the wide, semicircular bows, and until you are accustomed to it the 30ft or so of boat behind you can swing some way before you realise what is happening. In this case, keeping straight will be easier if you mark the windscreen and the forward cockpit coaming with sticky tape and use these marks for sighting the landscape.

STOPPING

The idea of not having brakes can fill the beginner with dread, and many avoid even considering the problem beforehand, a dangerous practice which usually results in hitting something. You will have to stop sooner or later, and it is best to do it first on a wide, clear reach where you can concentrate on the manoeuvre rather than worry about the consequences of failure.

First, as an experiment, with the boat travelling at a fair speed, throttle down and go into neutral. The boat, far from stopping, will drift a considerable distance, becoming progressively more difficult to steer, until all control is lost. If the rudder is hardly moving through the water, there is little pressure on it even when set hard over, and consequently no turning effect is produced. Of course you must slow down before stopping, but you must retain full control throughout, by keeping the propeller turning so that there is always some water passing the rudder.

Bearing this in mind, start up again and reach a fair speed. Again throttle down, but remain in gear, and the boat will still be under your control. Now go into neutral, just for a couple of seconds to give the propeller shaft time to stop, then go astern (engage reverse). The boat will stop, and if it does not do so quickly enough, increase the engine speed. In any case, *remain in reverse until the boat has stopped.* Then throttle down and go into neutral promptly before you start travelling backwards.

In practice, you will usually find that the stern swings to one side when you go astern on the engine, due to a tendency for the propeller, when in reverse, to act as a paddlewheel. Some boats are more prone to this than others, and the swing, if any, will not unnaturally always be to the same side in any particular boat. Once you have discovered to which side, the swing can be corrected. At this stage, the boat will hardly be moving, so the rudder will be useless.

In an inboard-powered boat, the correction must be made before you even go astern, while the boat is still travelling ahead. If, for example, you know that your boat swings to port (ie the *stern* swings to starboard), briefly put on some *starboard* rudder which will cause the stern to swing to port, and *then* go astern. The paddlewheel effect is then spent in correcting the opposite swing which you had deliberately started, and the boat is more likely to stop straight.

With an outboard or outdrive, ensure that the propeller is straight before engaging reverse, otherwise it will pull the stern sideways in whichever direction it is pointing. Alternatively, this effect can be used to correct paddlewheeling without the necessity for precorrection as with an inboard.

All this may seem most complicated, which is why many people will not even attempt it, preferring to drift into a mooring or a lock and grab something or jump off before hitting anything. Yet, after a few tries you will surprise yourself and your crew by judging it just right, and it soon becomes second nature.

The above advice refers to a boat which is travelling straight when stopped, but if it is not going straight it will not stop straight either, but will instead perform a slow pirouette on the spot! After more experience, this effect can be used to advantage, but for now always straighten before stopping. After half an hour's practice at steering and stopping, you should be able to approach a mooring without major mishap.

TURNING

In *Holiday Cruising on Inland Waterways* it was shown that to turn a boat round on a narrow waterway without danger of fouling the propeller or rudder, it is safest either to get off and pull her round on ropes or to nose the bows into the bank and pivot her by working the engine gently ahead with the rudder hard over. This sounds easy, but it is not to be recommended until you are competent enough to stop your boat within an inch of the bank, as even a comparatively small bump can cause shattered nerves, not to mention crockery.

On a wide river many boats will be able to turn round in one move, without either hitting the banks or grounding. A boat does not have a definite turning circle as does a car, and as a general rule a short boat will turn more tightly than a longer one, though the design of the hull and the speed of the boat will make quite a difference. Most hulls tend to slip sideways through the water when turning at high speed. If the waterway is not wide enough for this it is possible to do a sort of floating three point turn, but take care not to go aground with the propeller or rudder, which can be seriously damaged quite easily. The rudder has little effect when reversing, so on an inboard boat most of the actual turning must be done while working ahead, and may require a number of runs to and fro. Do not become impatient and try to drive away before you have completed the turn; remember that the stern swings wide and could go aground.

COMING ALONGSIDE

If you have practised diligently, you should now be able to bring the boat safely alongside a mooring. This requires a combination of all you have learnt, and is fairly simple provided you think clearly what instructions to give the boat.

On flowing water, always moor head-to-stream, ie with the bows pointing upstream against the current. This prevents any floating weed or rubbish from collecting on the rudder or propeller, and permits the boat to ride more comfortably should the flow increase. On still water, come in head-to-wind for the same reason. It also makes the boat easier to handle, because if you have any appreciable stream or wind behind you, the stern may be swung round away from the bank. So if you are approaching the mooring from upstream (or upwind on still water), go a little beyond, round-up (turn round), and come in from downstream instead.

Get the crew to put out fenders on the appropriate side, so that if you do misjudge it there will be no damage. With a crew of two, one stands at each end holding the nearest line. Assuming that there is sufficient depth and no obstructions, it is easiest to come in from as near as possible to the bank. This avoids having to turn too much, which is where the beginner usually has trouble. Slow right down, but *keep in gear* as long as you want to travel ahead, otherwise you will be unable to steer properly. If minimum speed is still too fast, come out of gear but give little bursts ahead to provide some steering. On reaching the desired position close to the bank, come out of gear and stop by going astern, increasing engine speed if necessary, then go into neutral again.

The crew member at the bows, who is likely to be the first within range, jumps ashore as soon as he can do so safely, but *does not pull* his rope until the boat has been stopped, as this will cause the bows to hit the bank and the stern to swing out, wrecking an otherwise good manoeuvre. If the one at the stern can get ashore as well, perhaps by walking with his line towards the bows if they are closer to the bank, each can then pull his own end of the boat gently in to the bank. If there is only one person, he can either take both lines with him or a single one from a cleat amidships. Once the lines are ashore, you can switch off, tie up the boat with a line each end, using simple knots described later, and adjourn to the pub.

The beginner who can master some or all of the techniques in this short chapter in a few hours can be forgiven for congratulating himself. If you have not found it so easy, there is no disgrace: try again on your next opportunity, but do not proceed to anything more complicated, because everything else you will learn is based upon these. Many will be happy not to advance further, but it is to be hoped that you will be keen to become more proficient, and will soon no more dream of having people jumping about and pulling on ropes than of pushing your car sideways into a parking bay. You will place the boat exactly where you wish, mainly on the engine, and the crew will throw lines deftly over bollards (a useful accomplishment in locks) and tie off quickly and confidently without orders or arguments. Such confidence is really satisfying, sets higher standards for others, and makes boating safer for all.

EMERGENCY PROCEDURES

Although most people spend their entire boating life without facing a serious emergency it is vitally important to be ready for one should it occur. The less experience you have, the more necessary it is to know exactly what you should try to do—and it *might* happen on your first trip.

FIRE

At the first sign of smoke or smell of burning, take a dry powder extinguisher and investigate the source. Do not ventilate, as this could provide enough oxygen for smouldering material to burst into flames. Work systematically, as follows:

1. If there is flame, use the extinguisher at once, giving two-second bursts at the base of the flames to drive them back. Powder in the middle of the fire is wasted if the flames are still spreading outwards. Prolonged bursts waste powder and could leave insufficient to finish the job.

2 When the flames are out, or if there is no flame, remove the cause (eg move heater, disconnect faulty wiring, remove panelling to expose source of smoke, etc).
3 Cool the area with water (provided no hot oil or fat is present).
4 Ventilate to disperse smoke and poisonous PVC fumes.
5 Watch for re-ignition.
6 If the fire is not extinguished immediately, try to get the boat ashore clear of buildings, crops, cattle and other craft before stopping the engine. The fire brigade should be called if there is any chance of their reaching the scene (which is frequently not the case).

Electrical Fires

Smoke from behind the dashboard or other panelling probably betrays an electrical fire, caused by overheated wiring. Do not waste time in looking for the faulty circuit: stop the engine to kill the charging circuit and switch off at the main battery terminal switch (or remove the lead). Open up the panelling and proceed as above.

Fat Fires

Burning fat in a pan should be covered with a damp (NOT wet) cloth to exclude air, and the pan taken outside to cool. If this fails, or if the fire has already spread, use the dry powder extinguisher at once. NEVER use water, which will cause burning fat to spatter everywhere and set the whole area alight.

Engine Compartment Fires

Switch off engine, main power and fuel valves first if possible, to remove the cause and reduce the risk of explosion.

Self-contained Gas and Paraffin Appliances

Use the extinguisher at once as there is no way of cutting off the fuel remotely.

Cookers and other Fixed Appliances
Turn off the main gas or other fuel supply first.

If the fire seems to be getting out of control, get all non-swimmers into lifejackets. Do not try to take the boat ashore unless well clear of other craft, buildings, trees, crops, cattle, etc, and do not turn on fuel to restart the engine. You could drop the anchor to prevent the drifting boat from endangering other property. If there is no hope of controlling the fire, or risk of explosion of gas or fuel, throw all lifebelts, fenders and other buoyant equipment overboard, including the dinghy if there is time, and *abandon ship*. Do not open the sea cock and sink the boat in an effort to minimise the damage. You may succeed, but are likely to incur heavy salvage costs which may not be met by your insurance. Get everybody as far away from the boat as possible. Other craft may help you from the water, but *keep them away* from the burning vessel.

When a fire breaks out while you are moored near other craft, it will probably be safer to move them than your own boat. If it happens in a lock, get the crew on the lockside, *not* in the water, from which it is difficult to climb out. Thames locks have large extinguishers and the keepers are trained for such an emergency. Obey their instructions, but ignore advice from sightseers, who always feel they know best. Keep them out of the way at all costs.

If someone else's boat is on fire, offer assistance and your extinguishers, and to take off any crew not fighting the fire. Do not moor or tow alongside, and if your help is not wanted *keep out of the way* and stand-by at a safe distance. Circumstances change quickly in a fire.

Obviously, someone should call the fire brigade if there is some chance of their reaching the spot, but most waterways are pretty well inaccessible to a fire engine. Always report any fire aboard a boat to the navigation authority, who may want to inspect the craft to discover the cause, with a view to avoiding other fires.

MAN OVERBOARD

Most people fall overboard at some time, and when it happens recovery will be quicker if everybody acts in a pre-arranged manner.

The Victim

He/she should immediately attempt to stand up, which will be perfectly possible on many canals and in many parts of a river, or a tideway at low water. Failing this, he should swim for the bank, or if this is too distant, remain afloat where he fell.

Inform the Helmsman

Anyone who sees the accident must shout 'Man overboard'. *Never* use this expression in fun, nor say 'help' if you do not need it. This is an emergency: do not waste time saying 'Hey, George! Jim was walking round the deck when he tripped over a fender and fell off!'

Stop

Stop when clear of Jim, by going hard astern. If he is some yards back, keep going astern until within about 10ft, then stop the boat with a burst ahead. If there are other craft about, use navigation signals or any unofficial means to inform them what you are doing.

Throw a Lifebelt

Throw a lifebelt with lifeline attached, whether the victim can swim or not. Use this to haul him to the boat, then hang it over the side and tie off to a cleat to give a foothold, unless you have a boarding ladder.

Return

If you have already travelled some distance, go about as quickly as possible, warning other craft if necessary with the appropriate sound signal (these are described in Chapter nine). When you reach him, stop with him near the bows. Do not waste time coming head to stream: he will be drifting at the same speed as you. Help him aboard as before. If he is a non swimmer, he should of course be wearing a lifejacket. Do not jump into the water except as a last resort, as you are more use standing firmly on the deck. Do not let anybody use the engine if the person in the water is anywhere near the propeller.

After Recovery

Provided the person is little the worse for his experience, simply make him dry and warm, but if there is any doubt, particularly with children or elderly people, obtain medical advice as soon as possible. If he is not breathing, give artificial resuscitation by the mouth-to-mouth method, and continue until self breathing takes over or until medical help can be obtained. Cover with warm clothes or rugs to retain body heat, provided this does not interrupt resuscitation, and in all cases where this has been necessary the patient *must* be taken to hospital for thorough examination. Do not attempt to give drinks.

CHAPTER FOUR

TOWARDS COMPETENT BOATING

In mastering the basic manoeuvres so far described, the beginner will have learnt much about the unique relationship between a boat and the water, and their behaviour together. Only when this relationship is understood may more advanced manoeuvres, which depend upon it, be studied. This is a continuing process which begins with your first trip and is never really completed. There is always something to learn or to improve upon.

The hirer, who has a whole week's continuous practice, is likely to master basic handling more quickly than the novice owner who only goes for short, infrequent trips, and meanwhile forgets much of what he has learnt. The unfortunate tendency for owners to feel superior to those in hired craft is therefore frequently misplaced. Among both categories there are those who, to their dismay, never attain great competence as well as those who feel that it does not matter anyway, as long as they are enjoying themselves. The former usually accept gladly any advice from the more experienced, whilst the latter are distinguished by aggressively rejecting it, by total indifference, or by blaming their shortcomings on the boat.

Having taken the trouble to read this book, you are clearly keen to learn as much as possible, so let us consider basic work in a little more detail before proceeding further.

A word about narrow boats

The advice so far applies to all motor craft; but the traditional style narrow boat, even in a short version, has unique handling characteristics. It is very long for its beam, usually too long to turn on a canal except at a 'winding hole' provided for the purpose. It is very heavy for its size, usually equipped with a low-revving engine (and therefore very economical) and slow to react, particularly when stopping. It does not mind scraping locksides or the bottom. But manoeuvres like high-speed turns, emergency stops and overtaking are usually impracticable. To avoid boring repetition, these characteristics should be borne in mind and will not necessarily be mentioned when discussing manoeuvres in terms of other types of craft.

MORE ABOUT STEERING

Although most hulls tend to steer themselves once they are moving at reasonable speed through the water, the major factor in keeping an inboard engined boat straight is the pressure of water upon the rudder. This is pivoted at its forward edge, and when turned to one side, the water through which it is passing exerts a pressure on it which causes it to move sideways in the opposite direction. As the boat is floating freely, this induces it to pivot somewhere in the middle so that the bows move sideways in the opposite direction to the stern, and therefore in the same direction as the rudder was moved. To stop this motion, it is not always sufficient to return the rudder amidships, and a certain amount of opposite pressure on the rudder is first necessary.

The faster the boat is travelling, the greater will be the pressure of water on the rudder, and the greater will be both the turning effect and the subsequent straightening effect of the rudder. Conversely at very low speeds, the rudder must be put over a long way to have much effect, and when stationary it will of course have none at all.

A boat with an outboard or outdrive does not normally have a separate rudder, though one is obtainable for fixing to the unit to enable the boat to be steered when moving with the propeller out of gear. Normally the boat is steered by swivelling the unit sideways to push at an oblique angle. This makes very little difference to the process of steering, though there are advantages and drawbacks to each system, which will be discussed in due course.

In a boat with a good keel, the tendency to veer from side to side will be less noticeable than with a comparatively smooth bottomed hull. Some lightweight glassfibre hulls have few fore-and-aft projections on the bottom, any so-called keel being little more than a slight ridge to strengthen a thin bottom. With such a boat, it is a good idea to fit a deeper, false keel, but even without this it can be steered straight in calm conditions, though loose or sloppy steering makes any boat more difficult to handle.

Wind

A strong crosswind tends to blow a boat bodily sideways, an effect which increases with the ratio of the height of superstructure to the draught of the hull. On a sailing craft the deep keel or centreboard largely prevents this, but the motor boat skipper must hold the helm slightly against the wind to avoid being blown off course, so in strong winds the boat proceeds somewhat crabwise.

The rudder has the subsidiary effect of discouraging sideways slipping, but with an outboard or outdrive you are denied this benefit, and such craft are notoriously difficult to handle in windy conditions.

Manufacturers of modern mass-produced cruisers seem more preoccupied with speed than with good handling characteristics, and there are very few today with even a nominal keel of, say, 4in. As it is easier to install an outdrive on such a hull than a conventional propeller and rudder, they are totally unsuitable for use in windy conditions on a confined waterway.

The long narrow boat is badly affected by wind, and it can become impossible to navigate a very narrow waterway unless the crew hold the bows against the wind, either with a line from the windward bank or a pole to the leeward bank.

Where there is any appreciable wind, there will also be waves,

Plate 6 (*above*) Approach a lock as straight as possible with ropes ready, and move well up to leave room for others;
Plate 7 (*below*) A common mistake is to tie up the bows before the boat has stopped. Use of reverse gear or the stern rope to stop the boat will prevent the stern from swinging dangerously

Plate 8 It is often safer to throw a line over a bollard than to jump ashore. (*above*) Hold the end of the line in the hand farthest from the cleat, the coil in the other, and *Plate 9* (*below*) throw the whole coil beyond the bollard then take in the surplus

which can push a small boat around. A study of how the boat behaves on the little waves on enclosed water will help to prepare you for the surprisingly large ones that can be thrown up on a wide tideway, or on the loch sections of the Caledonian Canal. You can even learn from the wash of other craft, and larger ones can considerably affect your progress.

Wash and Waves

The nature of the wash created by any boat depends mainly upon the shape of the hull. Broadly speaking, a short, fat, 'dumpy' hull will produce more wash than a long sleek, gently curved one. A boat with flat or snub bows, like a narrow boat, will push up a bigger bow-wash than one with a sharper angle to the bows, however long the hull. But the rest of the hull of the narrow boat, being of uniform shape throughout, will cause practically no additional wash, while the more rounded and ever-varying section of most river cruisers usually gives rise to additional waves at several points along the hull.

As the bows force their way through the water, they push out steep waves sideways, fairly close together and at an angle of about 45° to the hull (more or less according to the angle of the bows). Not all the water disturbed by the boat can escape in this way. Some is forced downwards and escapes backwards and outwards under the hull. As it does so, it pushes away the surrounding water, usually forming a trough close to the hull and a further system of outward-travelling waves from near the stern. On a hull where the stern below the waterline is rounded or curved, the water alongside rushes in to occupy the space vacated by the passing hull, and usually forms a trough and further waves as it does so. Finally, at the stern, these two opposing masses of water meet, together with the water moving backwards from underneath the hull (now assisted by the thrust of the propeller), and all combine to throw up a series of long waves just astern of the boat and at right angles to its course. This entire wash system keeps pace with the boat, and it is sometimes difficult to appreciate that this is only because it is being built up constantly by the boat, and at the other end each wave is breaking as it hits the banks or the shallower water.

You will appreciate from this that your boat creates a fair amount of disturbance as it passes, especially if you go fast, which is therefore forbidden on confined waterways including all canals and non-tidal rivers. Excessive wash not only upsets other people's boats, but also causes damage to the banks and erosion or silting of the bed as well. Even when they hit the bank, waves do not just disappear, but bounce off and travel back across the surface as 'backwash'.

When meeting the diagonal portion of a heavy wash, a boat tends to shy away from the crests and 'lean' into the troughs. If the helm is held still, the boat may simply zigzag a little but the average course remain unchanged, but with a little experience you can learn to steer a little into each wave and away from the troughs, thus maintaining a straight course. On passing from the other boat's bow wash into the screw wash, try to take this head-on to avoid bouncing off sideways and having to correct. Again, lessons learnt here can make all the difference to comfort and even safety in the big, confused waves of open water.

When meeting large commercial craft (or smaller ones going too fast) on a narrow waterway, the bow wash can carry the unwary towards the shallows at the edge. Then, the force of the backwards-moving water in the restricted space around the hull has the effect of drawing water *away* from the sides of the waterway, which can leave you on the 'putty'. To avoid this, steer closer to the other craft than to the bank, but take care not to be drawn towards it.

On busy non-commercial waterways like the Broads and Thames, cruisers often travel in all directions and quite fast. Their wash combines to give generally confused water which becomes quite choppy in a breeze. In a small boat, it is enjoyable as well as educational to judge how to take each wave, as well as concentrating on missing everybody else.

A different technique is necessary when travelling with instead of against large waves. Practise this by following another boat closely, riding on his screw wash. The boat will tend to sit at the bottom of a trough, held back by the wave ahead and pushed on by the one astern. Often, engine speed may be increased or decreased considerably without losing station, a fact which can assist with fuel economy. To overtake will need a fair amount of power, and before doing so you must take into consideration the speed of the other boat, the power of your own, the available width of the channel, the presence of other traffic and the fact that the vessel you are overtaking is under no obligation to move over or slow down for you.

Pull to one side and increase speed. You enter the diagonal wash from the quarter, and it takes some time to climb each wave, the boat trying to slip along the trough towards the other boat. Once the bows reach the crest, the boat pulls away towards the next trough. Learn to anticipate these swings, and to correct them before they actually occur, which is simply an extension of the method of keeping straight in a flat calm.

Never allow the boat to come broadside-on to the waves. Apart from being most uncomfortable, there would be a danger of capsizing under the rough conditions for which you are practising.

Bends and Turns

Although an aft steering position makes it easy to keep straight, both forward and aft positions require different techniques for negotiating bends and manoeuvring. In a restricted channel, anyone steering a forward-control cruiser who is unused to them, is likely to turn too late. While he is keeping the bows in the centre or even seeking deeper water towards the outside of the bend, the stern swings wide and could run aground. To avoid this, turn into the bend as soon as you can see that it is clear.

On a long narrow boat, you can see the first time you use the tiller that the bows and stern move bodily sideways in opposite directions, the boat pivoting somewhere ahead of the middle. It is easy to steer into the bend too early, with the risk of the bows cutting the bend and grounding. You must know where she pivots and keep *that* part in the middle of the channel, when the bows should cut the bend just enough to prevent the stern from hitting the opposite bank, though there may be precious little room either side. The observant beginner will quickly master the technique for either position, though these problems hardly arise on a boat with a steering position amidships. Being roughly where the boat will pivot, the skipper has only to put *himself* on the right line, and can largely forget his bows and stern except in really restricted conditions. This arrangement also has the advantage of dividing the accommodation into separate cabins fore and aft, a boon to those with small children to bed down early.

The turning characteristics of boats, like everything else afloat, depend on many factors, some of which have already been covered: hull shape, depth of keel, length, size and position of rudder, etc. A boat with a deep 'V' shape forward and an almost flat bottom aft will pivot nearer its bows and the stern slide round easily, while one with a deep full-length keel will take longer. At high speed, however, the former craft might have so little of its bows in the water that it slips bodily sideways, making a much wider turn. Most inland cruisers, top-heavy, with shallow or rounded bottoms, heel alarmingly towards the outside of a sharp turn, while a speedboat with no high superstructure, a deep 'V' bottom and propellers and rudders dug deeply into the water providing leverage, will lean into its turn. Indeed, almost any powerful boat will do so a little at first, before heeling outwards.

Most cruisers can turn more tightly at lower speeds, a higher speed causing loss of time due to the extra distance covered through slipping sideways. The technique for turning about quickly in an emergency is therefore a combination of the two. First, put the helm hard over and shut down the throttle. As the bows drop, the stern rises and begins to skate round. After a couple of seconds, open the throttle again, giving the stern a powerful kick round without increasing the speed through the water too much. Despite the time taken in slowing down, the result is a really fast turn.

This manoeuvre is obviously limited to wide rivers and the Broads. If you are going against any appreciable stream, it will assist if you turn from the side towards the centre (or towards the outside of a bend), while a following stream will help to push your stern round if you turn towards the slacker water at the edge. In strong stream or windy conditions, never turn just upstream (or upwind) of bridges, weirs or moored craft as you will be swept sideways and may collide with them.

TWIN ENGINES

To have twin engines on a craft used exclusively on inland waterways is probably an extravagance. They burn double the fuel for a little extra power; but they are sometimes helpful in manoeuvring. Where there is room to turn in one go, it is quickest to do so as just described. In addition, reversing the inside engine will help her to spin. If there is less room, stop either by reversing both engines, or by reversing only one and putting the other in neutral to start her swinging as she stops. Then, by working ahead on one and astern on the other, turn her in her own length.

All the remarks about turning a single-screw boat apply also to outboards and outdrives. The advantages of outboard engines are that they make a boat easy to steer in reverse, and can be tilted to remove weeds or other rubbish. Used as twins, they provide little benefit except for extra power (which you do not need on speed-restricted waters) and a spare in case of breakdown (which when it happens causes most people to complain that 'she won't handle on only one'). For manoeuvring purposes, they do not handle as well as twin inboards, partly because of the lack of rudders, and partly because they are rarely separated by a keel and cannot function independently, tending just to churn up the water when used in opposite directions.

It is desirable for twin engines to be 'handed', ie arranged for the propellers to rotate in opposite directions when in the same gear. The port propeller usually rotates anticlockwise when running ahead, and the starboard clockwise, which when used in opposite directions for manoeuvring produces a considerable paddlewheel action to assist, and of course eliminates the effect when going straight.

STOPPING

Practise stopping in open water as described in Chapter three. A boat with handed twin engines is more likely to stop straight, if you use both equally. In an inboard, the harder you go astern, the greater will be the tendency for the stern to swing round, and the greater must be the pre-correction. Boating is a leisurely pastime, and it is sheer exhibitionism to throw a launch all over the water, driving hard into locks and then having to go full astern to stop; but an emergency stop is sometimes necessary, and there is certainly a case for adopting fairly positive techniques when using a busy waterway like the Thames. If too many people waste time drifting into locks with the engine switched off, or towing in on lines, the result is long queues of angry and impatient people.

There is no need to throw the boat about, but you must handle it efficiently. Practise stopping at all speeds, finding out how long it takes and how the boat behaves. Try anchoring a plastic fender as a marker buoy. You then approach this at various speeds and aim to stop exactly alongside the buoy, in as straight a line as possible and under full control. Use this arrangement also to practise stopping when not going straight. You can always straighten a boat before stopping, if there is time, but there are occasions when it is useful to be able to stop in an arc, particularly when you have to round-up to approach a mooring head-to-stream, or even to approach a mooring from a slight angle. To try approaching a real bank at an angle and at any speed without previous practice is likely to result in a hefty collision. If using a buoy for this, make sure that there is no spare rope floating around to foul the propeller; and if you do hit the buoy do so with your engine in neutral.

Approach the make-believe bank at an angle, then at the last moment turn away, and go astern on the engine fairly hard as in Fig 7 (page 62). Although the boat will stop, it will remain turning on the spot, and with luck or judgement will float sideways into the right position. If you turn away too soon, you will either miss altogether, or reach the bank only with your stern. If in addition you reverse too soon, you will not even reach the bank. Turning away too late will almost certainly cause you to ram the bank, unless you quickly reverse hard, stopping bows-to the bank. Of course, if you were approaching a real bank, which is considered in Chapter five, the situation could be saved by the prompt use of lines and fenders, and you might even be able to give the impression that that was what you meant to do all along!

With twin inboard engines go astern on the engine away from the bank, and ahead on the other. Turn the rudder away from the bank to assist; and since you are stopping the boat as well as turning it, you will need plenty of 'astern' and not too much 'ahead'.

With outboard or outdrive installations, you effect the manoeuvre in yet a third way. Approach as before, turning away at the last moment, then whilst in neutral quickly turn the propellers *towards* the bank and go astern (on both if twins), stopping the boat and pulling in the stern in one move. Note that you cannot, as with twin inboards, go ahead on the inner engine to assist, because with the propellers turned towards the bank, its thrust would be sufficient to push her out whatever the other engine was doing. This emphasises that outboards used as twins do not necessarily improve a boat's handling characteristics.

CHAPTER FIVE

MOORING

The first time you have to bring a boat alongside a mooring will probably be long before you have had time to practise the manoeuvres just described. It will probably be a case of getting as close as you can to the bank and having the crew jump for it with lines. They must beware, however, for one or more people jumping from even a fairly large boat can propel it further away from the bank, and many is the ducking that has been had that way!

APPROACHING A MOORING

On flowing water always moor head-to-stream as already stated, and if the proposed mooring is unfamiliar you must first decide on a stretch of bank that looks suitable: a convenient height for going ashore, not unsafe due to undermining by water rats or wash, and without either too many roots sticking out to damage the boat or nettles to damage you. There must be sufficient depth of water (and headroom under trees) to allow for a change in level of a foot or so, a greater rise or fall being unlikely on a non-tidal waterway except on certain rivers after prolonged rainfall. The Warwickshire Avon is an example where the level can rise rapidly by several feet, due to its solid overfall-type weirs with no sluice gates to pass excess water. By contrast, a big river like the Thames, with its large adjustable weirs always manned, and with a constant watch kept on water levels on every reach, can pass a considerable quantity of 'landwater' before its levels rise to any extent. A river flowing fast assumes a steeper gradient, and will therefore rise more just below a weir than above.

On canals, changes in water level are unlikely except on very short pounds (the sections between locks), where mooring should be avoided. A narrow boat often has to run aground and moor a few feet from the bank, in any case.

Other places to avoid when mooring are in the vicinity of locks and bridges where you may obstruct other craft, and on a bend where long craft need room for the stern to swing, and where the inside may be too shallow anyway. Never tie up to private land, even fields and islands, without permission unless it is clearly a recognised mooring. Most waterways have a towpath to one side, and in the absence of horse-drawn traffic mooring is normally permitted to this subject to local requirements. There are many places, usually well marked, where local or navigation authorities have improved the banks for the purpose, and here mooring is sometimes subject to a small fee. Local information is obtainable from maps, guides or natives.

Slow right down, and if the current permits, approach at an angle of about 45°: it may be shallow, and it is better to touch bottom with the bows than to risk damaging the propeller. A crew member forward could usefully 'sound' for depth with a boathook or shaft, and it is useful to have one marked off in feet or with the depth required for your sterngear.

On nearing the bank, take the engine right out of gear and just give the occasional touch ahead to keep the boat moving and to steer, so that there will be no damage even if the propeller does just touch bottom. By feeling around with your shaft, you might well be able to find a deep enough bit for the stern, and if the bottom proves to be deep soft mud, damage is unlikely in any case. Once the bows are in, the crew can go ashore with lines. Switch off the engine, if water-cooled, to avoid sucking weeds and mud into the cooling system. Any blockage will remain undiscovered until you are under way again, when the engine may overheat and possibly seize. These may also be caused by labouring due to weed on the propeller. Train yourself to check that the cooling water is coming out every time you get under way, and check the engine temperature gauge periodically for overheating (you can usually smell it too).

Nobody will scorn you for relying on lines in unknown terrain instead of the engine, but at proper moorings there will almost certainly be enough depth and you should be able to approach straight, almost parallel to the bank until about a foot away, and then stop by going astern just as you practised in midstream. Crew and lines can then be put ashore in safety.

If you cannot find a landing clear enough to approach in this way, you will be obliged to come in at an angle (Fig 7). Approach

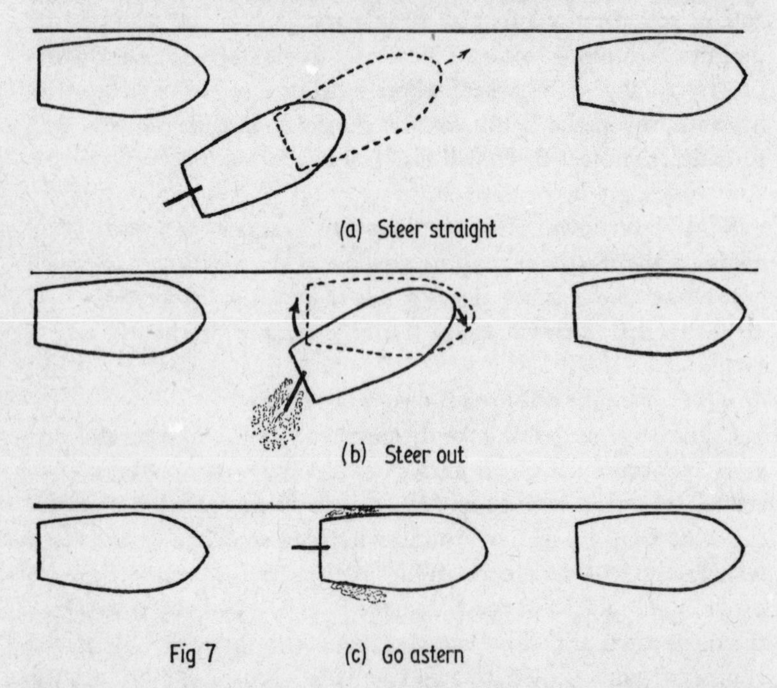

Fig 7

just far enough out to clear other moored boats and just fast enough to steer, aiming beyond the centre of the available space. Keep in gear until the last possible moment to retain steering way, and put the wheel hard over away from the landing in time to avoid hitting it. Give a little burst ahead to kick the stern in, then go astern hard enough to stop her. With an outboard or outdrive, you *must* turn the helm towards the bank before doing this.

There is no point in anyone stepping ashore without a line, or there is a delay whilst somebody else throws one and the possibility of missing anyway. If you have managed to get the bows in but have 'lost' the stern, have the crew put out the forward line and make it fast working backwards (a 'backspring'). Then, with the helm *away* from the bank and the boat well fended, go carefully *ahead*. Water thrown from the propeller, deflected by the rudder on an inboard, pushes the stern sideways to the wharf, the boat pivoting on its forward line (Fig 8). The bows must not be tied too closely, or they will be unable to move out as the stern moves in. With an outboard, the same result is achieved by working the forward line ahead (a 'forespring'), turning the propeller *towards* the wharf, and going *astern*. Please note that you cannot normally do this in an inboard unless the paddle-wheel effect of the propeller is considerable, and even then it will only work when coming in on one side.

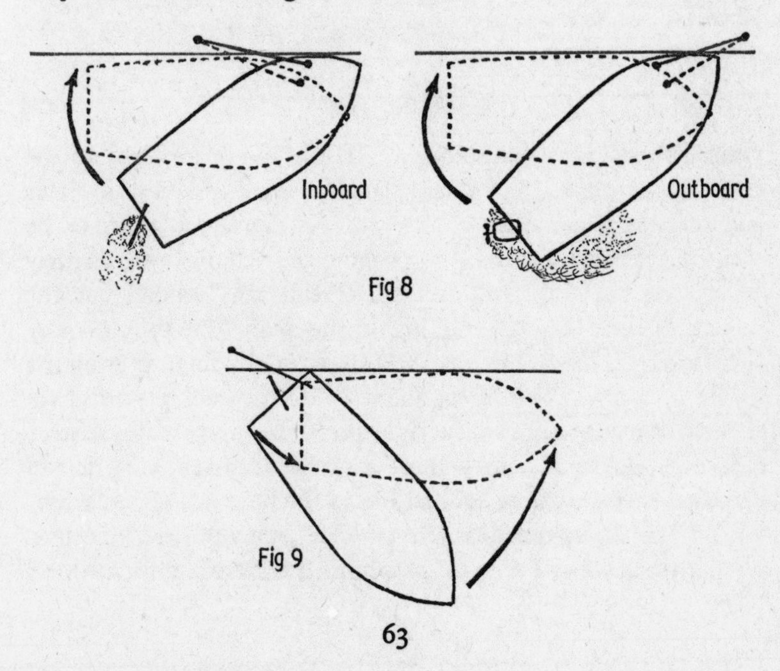

Fig 8

Fig 9

It is difficult to manoeuvre a boat in reverse because you have no control over the bows. Do not try reversing into a mooring space, or you will probably finish with your stern by the wharf but no means of getting the bows in. This situation may also be the result of turning away too soon when approaching a mooring ahead. If it happens, run a backspring from a cleat or fairlead on the quarter nearest the bank to a suitable fixed point ashore. Make it fast, and whether in an inboard or an outboard, put the wheel slightly towards the bank and go ahead (Fig 9). The boat will pivot on its line and come nicely alongside provided there is not a strong head- or cross-wind or stream. In this case you will either have to pull the bows in on a line or drive away and try again.

In a really strong stream, move ahead until abreast of the mooring space, and slow down until you maintain this position against the stream. A small alteration of the helm will slip you bodily broadside into the space, and the crew must make fast at once with the head line. Do not let anybody jump, even a short distance, under these conditions as it is difficult to recover anyone who falls into fast water.

MAKING FAST

Once alongside, tie up in such a way that the boat is free to ride vertically on the wash of passing boats or slight variations in water level, yet not so loosely that it can run back and forth or be thrown against the bank. Any pronounced lengthways run may cause scraping of the hull unless it is really well fended, and the fraying of lines through rubbing on the quay. The simplest way to make fast is to put out head and stern lines from fittings on the landward side of the boat, at about 45° to the bank as in Fig 10. If the bollards are not in the right positions, perhaps because of other moored craft, extra lines may be required in order to persuade them to do the job. In Fig 11 the boat would run astern but for the forespring 'a'. Alternatively, run the head line to a more distant bollard, line 'b' becoming a backspring to keep the

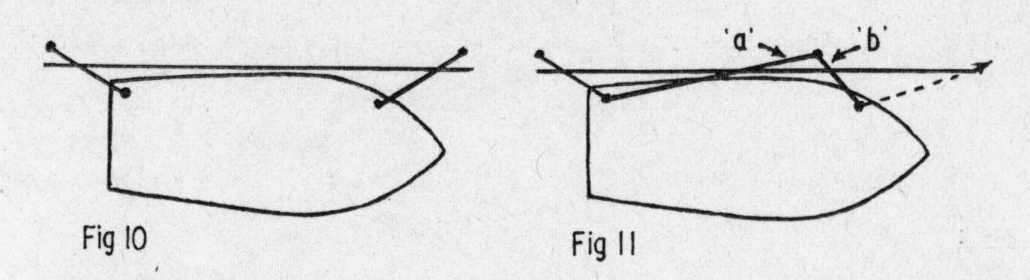

Fig 10 Fig 11

bows in. This method can of course equally be applied to the opposite end of the boat as necessary.

Should the bollards be too far apart for the lines to hold the boat snugly to the wharf, it will help to run them from the outside fittings as in Fig 12, which also shows two methods of preventing excessive fore-and-aft movement either by returning the lines from the shore to the inside fittings (lines 'a') or by running springs to a central bollard (lines 'b').

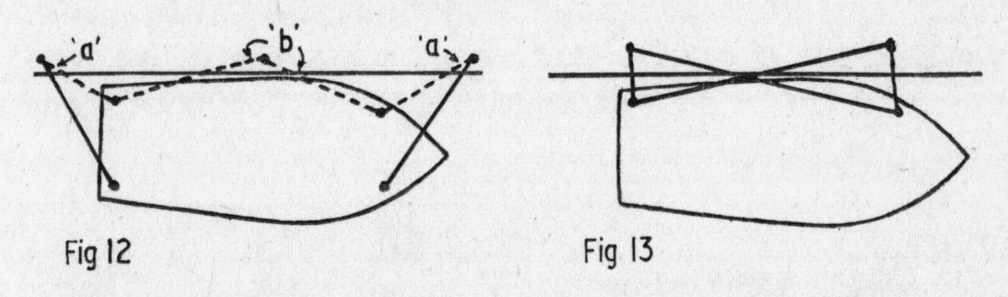

Fig 12 Fig 13

Where the only available bollards occur right opposite the cleats, tie off both the head and stern lines ashore, then return them as springs to the opposite ends of the boat (Fig 13). To run lines to more distant bollards would serve little purpose and could obstruct their use by other craft, clearly unreasonable on a busy mooring.

With mooring cleats positioned along the hull, it is usually easy to work out a formula to satisfy your requirements. Do not be afraid to use a different arrangement at each end of the boat if this seems useful. In Fig 14, the headline and spring together are necessary because of the awkward position of the bollard, whilst the stern line if run from the outside quarter will do its job quite adequately unaided.

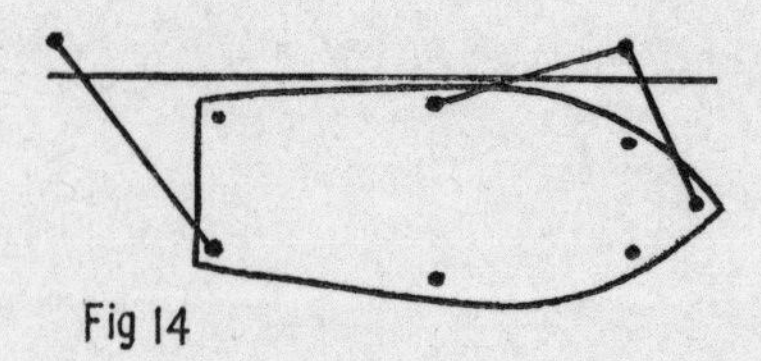

Fig 14

On a craft with fairly straight sides, it is often adequate to moor temporarily with a single line amidships, called a 'breast line'. The boat cannot turn and chafe due to its straight sides. Regrettably, however, modern canal boats are rarely fitted with additional cleats along the sides for mooring purposes, which would surely be a point to raise when having one built. Many builders of so-called traditional style craft are prepared to ruin the lines of their boats by skimping on steel or on work, and by introducing long after-decks where the traditional cabin should be because this is more convenient for pleasure purposes; yet the idea of providing for other requirements of the pleasure boat, like cleats and somewhere to stow an anchor and chain, does not seem to occur to anybody.

Although most references have been to the use of bollards, as a matter of convenience, the advice holds good for all mooring devices which may be provided. When mooring away from home, you may have to use your own mooring pegs, and subject to suitable terrain, these may be placed where you wish for best results. Do not put them too close to the edge, which can cause the bank to fall away, spoiling it and setting you adrift; but equally they must not be far enough back to interfere with use of the towpath by walkers. Two or three feet back should be sufficient, and if there is any danger of people tripping over pegs or ropes, mark them with white cloths. Never take lines right across the towpath to distant trees or fences. Angle straight pegs slightly away from the boat so that the strain holds them down instead of pulling them out.

It is not always possible to find an ideal mooring, and you may have to make do with a shallow one or with roots sticking out from the bank. Here, use an anchor or two over the side to hold you away from danger. Overhanging branches can sometimes be useful for this too, but beware sudden changes in water level on rivers prone to them. Fig 15 shows a typical situation: to arrange a mooring is only a matter of *thinking* how the boat is to be held, then acting on your conclusions. It is not just a matter of making sure that the boat does not float away, yet do not run lines in all directions unless they are necessary, considering the prevailing conditions of wind, stream, wash and others who may wish to share the mooring.

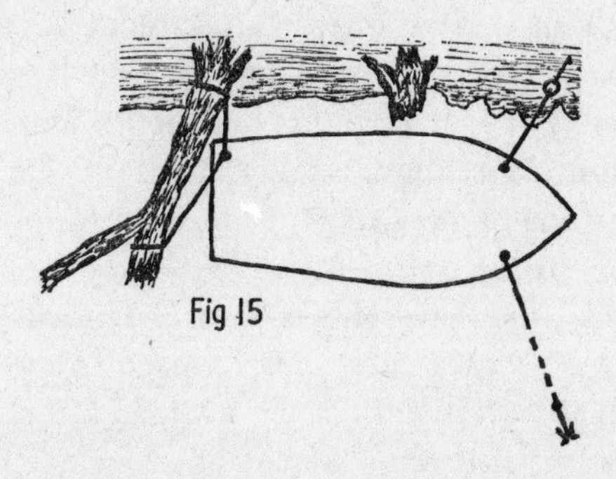

Fig 15

Mooring a narrow boat on a canal demands a different technique. There is rarely sufficient room to turn round, and often insufficient water to come close to the bank. Run the bows to the bank and put ashore two crew with mooring pegs and the bow rope. Throw the stern rope to one, put the rudder hard over away from the bank, and go full ahead to slide the stern in. The bows will probably come out slightly, and the boat will find a position with the stern (which draws more water) rather further out than the bows. Give a touch astern if she is moving ahead, and tie up with both lines tight and at an angle of 45° to the hull. The gangplank may be needed.

Having made fast satisfactorily, stop the engine. It is unwise to do this at an earlier stage, unless the water is shallow as already mentioned, just in case the mooring suddenly proves to be unsuitable. Check for bulls, wasps' nests and similar unpleasant discoveries before driving in mooring pegs!

TIDEWAY MOORING

Mooring on a tideway is generally inadvisable except to a floating pontoon or mooring buoy, or to piles with rings free to slip vertically on bars. Even then, do obtain local advice. Not only do the edges usually dry out at low water, but sometimes even pontoons and piles are left high and dry. A craft with a flat bottom or otherwise built for beaching may be dried out on a suitable foreshore without taking harm, but without advice you might select a spot with a steep slope, rocks or really deep mud. If you anchor in emergency, 'sound' for the depth and nature of the bottom, and if in doubt move further out as the tide falls.

To use a floating landing stage, come in head-to-tide and make fast with good, strong lines working well ahead and astern, leave plenty of slack, and have the boat well fended. On the tidal Thames, there are several such 'piers' at useful intervals where it is usually possible to arrange to lie for a while, but elsewhere there are all too few.

If you propose to leave the boat at a deep-water wharf for any length of time, you *must* find out how much the tide will rise or fall in that time and make the necessary provision when setting your lines. It is best if possible to leave someone aboard to check and adjust the lines as necessary. If this is not convenient, put out really long lines head and stern so that there will be sufficient slack for the change in level, yet enough tension to hold the boat still. As lines set in this way will not hold her particularly close, she must be very well fended. If for example the tidal range is 15ft, it is not excessive to put out 60ft or more at each end. After setting the lines taut, pay out another 10ft to give sufficient slack. It is not a bad idea to attach weights to the centres of the lines to keep them taut—5lb will do. If the boat has a rudder, set the helm towards the wharf, which will keep the uptide end in

Plate 10 (above, left) Make sure in a lock that the strain of the boat cannot trap the 'running' end of a rope, particularly on bollards with cross pins; *Plate 11 (above, right)* The Bargee's Hitch cannot slip or pull tight, and can always be released; *Plate 12 (below)* If possible, occupy the space beside a previous boat in a lock, as a following craft may be too large, wasting space and causing others to be 'locked out'

Plate 13 (above) The almost flat bottoms and shallow draught of most small glassfibre hulls give indifferent handling, especially with outboards and particularly when windy;
Plate 14 (below) In contrast the deep rudder, keel and bilge keels of this boat give excellent stability, steering and beaching characteristics

whichever way the tide is running and prevent her from being thrown hard against the wharf.

When using piles or buoys, it is usually better to lie between two rather than to hang by the head line from only one. Approach head to tide, and pass a long head line *once* through the ring and back to the boat. Take a turn on the samson post and pay out enough line for the pile astern to be reached. Use reverse if necessary. Pass the stern line once through the ring there and back to the boat, then haul in the head line and pay out the stern one to centre the boat between the piles, where she will ride comfortably even when the tide turns.

Make sure before using a buoy that it *is* for mooring and not a channel marker or someone's anchor buoy! If possible, ask permission, to avoid inconveniencing the owner should he return. All buoys belong to *someone*, and at least there may be a small charge payable.

LEAVING A MOORING

Even on a straight, clear wharf you cannot just let go and drive away. You must first get one end or other of the boat pointing away from the wharf, either by pushing off as already described (which is perfectly satisfactory in a light boat) or with the engine (which is more fun in any boat). Otherwise, when you try to turn away, the stern swings towards the wharf and hits it, possibly hard enough to bounce off, pivoting the boat so that the bows hit the wharf next.

With an outboard, you pull the stern out by turning the helm away from the wharf and going astern until you are clear enough to drive off ahead. In an inboard, put the rudder towards the wharf whilst still stationary, and give a short burst ahead to kick the stern out. The boat should not move ahead far, but if there is a danger of hitting the craft ahead, use the head line as a backspring as in Fig 8 (page 63), an exact reversal of coming alongside. To make the bows come out on the engine, make fast the stern with a forespring from the inside quarter and go astern. Stop, let go the spring quickly and drive away before the stream can turn you right round. If the tide has turned, leaving you stern-to-tide, you may not be able to get the bows out in this way, and must either push out the bows with a shaft before driving out fast to avoid being swept into other craft, or turn the boat on the mooring to face the tide.

'Winding', as this is called, is done as follows. Run a head line from the offshore cleat, round the bows and secure it ashore opposite the stern. Set fenders on the offshore side, start the engine and let go all other lines. Put the helm *towards* the wharf if necessary and kick the stern out as before (Fig 16a). As the

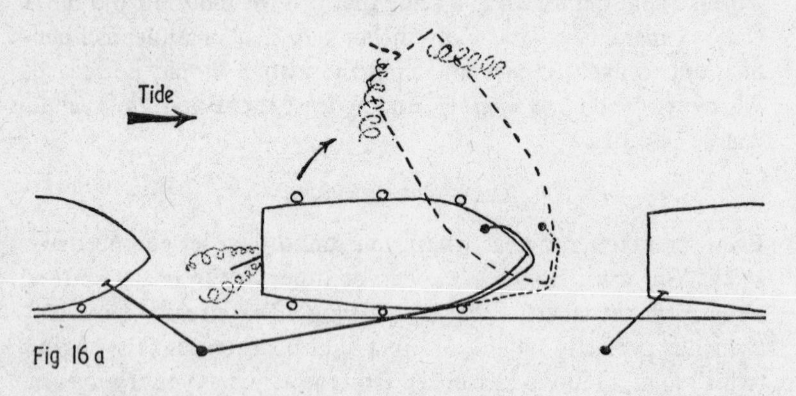

Fig 16 a

stern swings out and round on the tide, give an occasional touch astern to keep the bows clear of the wharf, until the turn is about threequarters completed. Still with the helm in the same position (which will now have become *away* from the wharf), go ahead (Fig 16b), and steer the boat up to the original mooring whilst the crew shorten the head line (this is not necessary if the down-tide part of the wharf is vacant). You can now get away head to tide.

To leave buoys or piles with a following tide, the safest procedure will be dictated by the strength of the tide and the space between the piles or other moored craft. Let go the head line first and go astern whilst shortening the after line to give the maximum room for manoeuvre. Again, either let go and drive out fast ahead,

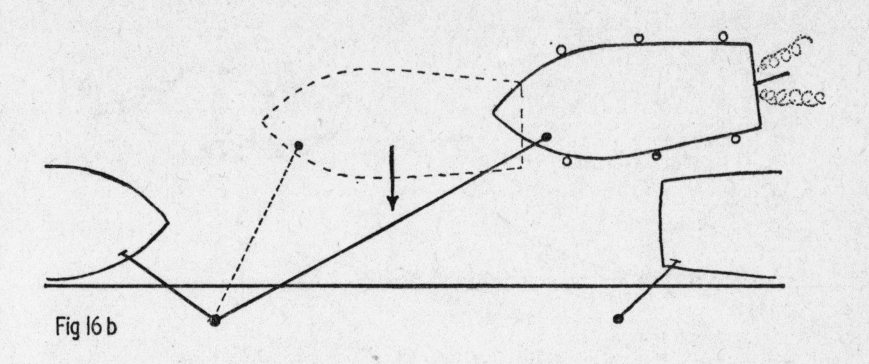

Fig 16 b

or wind the boat by running a head line back to the after pile, letting the tide swing her as before.

ANCHORING

One of the reasons for using a tideway at all is to reach other waterways which join it. Entry to a non-tidal waterway is always by a lock, which is generally only usable at certain states of the tide. It is not always possible to time your arrival to coincide with these, particularly if you have had to wait at another lock to enter the tideway; and unless there happens to be a good mooring, you will have to wait at anchor. On any flowing water, the anchor may also be needed in the event of a breakdown.

It is useless just to lower an anchor over the bows until it touches the bottom, and then expect it to hold. Most anchors rely on digging themselves into the bed of the river, and cannot do so if the buoyancy of the boat is tending to lift them. Use a long rope, at least three times the depth of the water, to reduce the angle sufficiently to allow the anchor to grip; a length of chain between the anchor and the rope, or chain throughout, will also help to hold it down (Fig 17).

If going with the stream or tide, round-up into it before dropping the anchor, otherwise the boat will over-ride the anchor and the rope could foul the propeller. Naturally, if you have

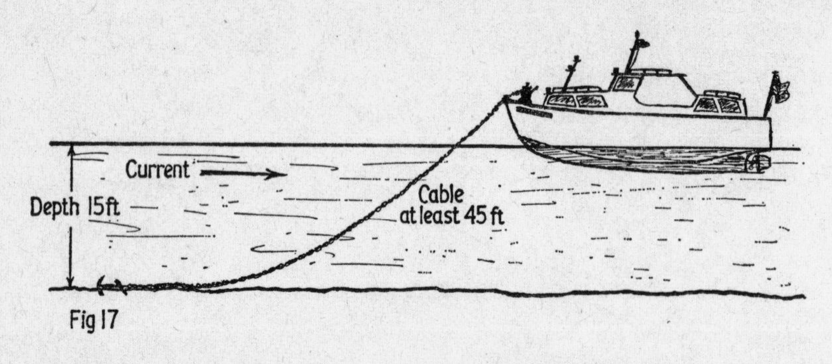

Fig 17

broken down, this will not be possible, but there will be little danger of fouling the stationary propeller anyway. Even if you are not using all your cable, the end of it must always be secured to the boat for safety.

Before letting go the anchor, if possible ascertain the depth of the water either with a long pole, a weighted line marked at intervals of a fathom (6ft) or perhaps 10ft, or by lowering the anchor itself and noting the amount of line paid out. Then pay out three times the depth of the water, letting the boat drop gently astern until the anchor bites. Never try to take the strain with the hands, particularly if out of control, but take a turn on the main cleat or samson post. When the anchor bites, slow the boat by tightening this turn, and when you have stopped the boat and paid out the correct length of line, tie-off and check that it is holding by watching a reference point ashore. A careful pull on the line will confirm the matter.

A dragging anchor may be corrected by paying out more cable, but persistent dragging indicates that the anchor is either unsuitable for the bed, too light for the boat, or fouled by its own line and lying incorrectly. If all else fails, haul up and try again, and if you suspect insufficient weight, tie the steel mallet to the cable a foot or so above the anchor.

While lying at anchor, steer the boat if necessary to prevent her from swinging into the path of passing traffic or towards the edge and stranding. This swinging can be reduced as the tide falls by shortening the cable, being careful to maintain the 3:1 ratio to the depth. When the tide turns, as it may quite abruptly, it will push the boat towards and past the anchor, which may become dislodged as it turns under the reversed strain, and must be checked. Any line taken in must be paid out again as the tide rises.

If a tidal bore or eagre is expected, get under way beforehand and meet it head-on in midstream. If broken down, either quant or paddle the boat around to face downstream before it arrives, possibly rigging an additional anchor from the stern to hold this position. Pay out twice the normal length of anchor cable, and have *everybody* in lifejackets. Bores and other tideway matters are discussed fully in Chapter eight.

Before taking in the anchor, start the engine and warm it up until it can be relied upon not to stall. Then haul in the anchor line, pulling the boat ahead (help with the engine in fast water), and when the line is vertical a sharp pull should break-out the anchor from the bed. Haul it up carefully so as to avoid putting it through the bottom of the boat.

You may be unfortunate enough to foul the anchor by getting it entangled amongst rubbish, old ropes or mooring chains, or even under a lump of stone or waterlogged timber. If it does not break-out fairly easily, do not just pull harder, which could wedge it even more firmly. Try working the boat into a different position, letting out line as necessary, and pull from another angle. If the water is shallow enough, probing with a boathook might dislodge it, but only after all else fails is it advisable to try brute force, first by lifting or winching and finally by transferring the line to the stern and pulling in various directions on the engine.

In fast water, this is not easy. Use the helm to swing the boat slightly sideways, then drive ahead against the stream whilst the crew shortens the anchor line. As you pass the anchor, the crew transfer it to a stern cleat, let a little run out then snub it with another turn which should dislodge the anchor. Haul it in without stopping so that it streams clear of the propeller.

It is a common practice in coastal boating to provide a trip line, attached at one end to the crown of the anchor and at the other to a small buoy (a PVC fender will do), by which the anchor can be broken out more easily. It only needs to be about 1½ times the depth, and is paid out with the anchor line. To recover the anchor, drive carefully ahead, hauling in the slack anchor line, and pick up the buoy with a boathook. Use the trip line to break out the anchor, then take the weight on the anchor line and haul both aboard.

Because of the extra space and crew required, this procedure is rare on inland waterways, where serious fouling is unusual anyway, though it could be a wise precaution in the vicinity of old moorings and docks, where the remains of underwater constructions, chains, etc may still be encountered.

Do not anchor on a canal except with a mudweight, lest the flukes damage the puddled clay bottom and cause a leak.

CHAPTER SIX

ROPEWORK

It is not necessary to be able to tie complicated knots, far less to know their names, except as an exercise for your own enjoyment. The essence of good practical ropework lies in the ability to set lines to the best advantage, using only simple hitches which are quick, secure, yet easily undone however great the strain on them. Even so, a few unfamiliar terms will be required, which will warrant some explanation.

Ropes used aboard a boat are normally fixed at one end either to the boat or to some piece of equipment like a fender, while the other end is free. When making a knot or hitch, all the rope between that work and the fixed end is called the 'standing part' or 'standing end', and the length between the work and the free end the 'running part'. When practising at home, always tie one end to something first so that this situation prevails from the start.

ATTACHING LINES TO THE BOAT

For quick attachment to and removal from cleats, it is usual to splice or tie an eye in the standing end of a rope, and to back-splice or whip the running end to prevent fraying.

Eye Splice

Splicing a rope of the size recommended in Chapter two is fairly easy, and the eye splice is the simplest of all. For this reason, one often sees it used in both ends of a rope, but this can be dangerous as a loose eye is apt to catch on things while using the line. You will however see the crews of large commercial craft using heavy ropes with a large eye at one end which they throw deftly over a bollard or pile, up to 20ft away, then take a couple of turns on the bollard of their craft. Do not try this with your lighter lines, as the eye will not be stiff enough to remain open as it travels.

Most stranded ropes are 'hawser laid', ie with three strands twisted in a clockwise direction as illustrated in all the following diagrams. On four strand ('shroud laid') rope, the methods of splicing are much the same, and on a rope twisted in the opposite direction ('cable laid'), any splices must also be reversed.

To make an eye splice, first cut off any frayed ends so that you have three good strands to work on. Each can be tied with thin twine to prevent further fraying.

Carefully unstrand a few inches and lay this unstranded part back over the rope to form an eye of the size required, as in Fig 18 (i). Loosen the strands on the standing part where the end lies across it, then take the middle strand *b* and tuck it under the strand it lies on, against the lay of the rope (ii). Next take the right

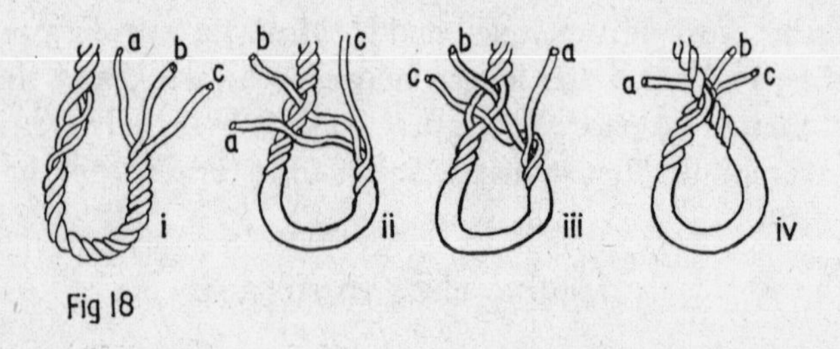

Fig 18

hand strand *c*, cross it under *b*, and tuck it under the next strand of the standing part to the left of *b* (iii). Turn the splice over, take the remaining strand *a* and tuck it under the third strand of the standing part, still against the lay of the rope (iv), so that the three ends stick out from beneath different strands at the same point of the rope. Now take each end strand in turn and pass it over the next strand and under the following one on the standing part, then repeat the procedure two or three times, working at right-angles to the lay and turning the work over as you go.

Then, with a sharp knife cut off the remaining ends, and roll the whole splice under your foot.

Crown Knot and Backsplice

Before you can work a backsplice, the end of the rope must be 'stopped' with a Crown Knot. Unstrand a few inches, tidying frayed ends, as in Fig 19 (i): take the right-hand strand *c*, pass it to the left between the other two in a large loop, and hold it in position; (ii) now bring the left-hand strand *a* up round that loop tightly, towards the right, thus holding the first loop in position, and hold it; (iii) finally, pass the remaining strand *b* over *a* and down through the first loop you made; (iv) and pull tight, still holding *a*. Pull *c* tight as well, then give all three strands a pull in turn to make the knot firm. You can now backsplice as described for the eye splice.

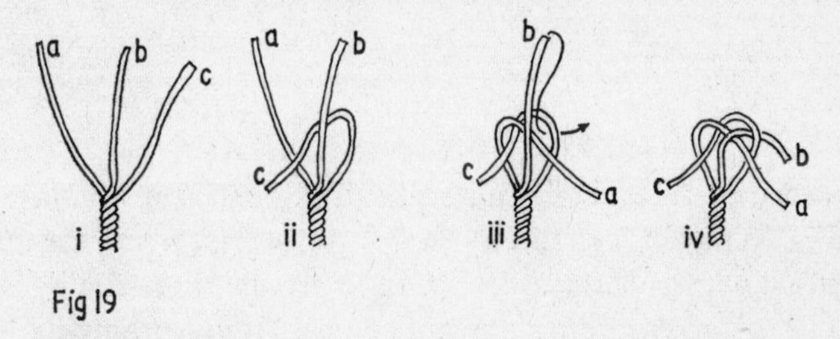

Fig 19

Whipping

Any line which is not spliced, including a woven line, must be whipped at its running end to prevent fraying or unstranding, even with some artificial fibres where it is possible to melt the end with a cigarette lighter and fuse the fibres together. Unlike a splice, a whipping is hardly fatter than the original line and is therefore unlikely to jam on fittings or in cracks and crevices in locksides.

Remove any frayed ends, then take a length of thin twine, and lay it along the rope for about two inches (Fig 20, (i)). Hold the ends of both together and start winding the twine tightly around the rope and itself, working *towards* the end of the rope (ii). After about six turns, hold the work tightly to prevent slipping, and lay a long loop of the twine over the work (iii). Then, using only the side of the loop marked 'a' in the diagram, continue with the tight turns towards the end of the rope, leaving the other side of the loop trapped underneath them. After a further six or so turns, hold the final turn tight and pull the running end of the twine so that the remainder of the loop is pulled inside the whipping (iv). Give a final pull to each end of the twine to ensure that they are taut, then cut them off short, taking care not to sever the whipping or the rope.

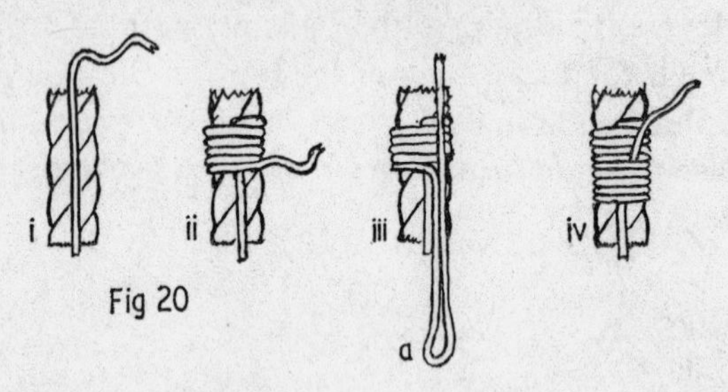

Fig 20

Seizing

Formed exactly as a whipping, this is a method of binding together two ropes. It would be used, for example, where the line is to be tied permanently, as in Fig 21 where the short end is seized to the running end to prevent the hitches from working loose.

Fig 21

Bowline

A rope should only be *tied* to a cleat if never required elsewhere and if there is still room on the cleat for tying off the running end. On a woven line, where an eyesplice is impractical, a neat, slip-proof eye can be tied using the Bowline (pronounced 'boe-lyn').

About sixteen inches from the end of the line (depending on the size of eye required) form a small loop (as in Fig 22 (i)) with the running end on top of the standing part. Hold it with finger and thumb of the left hand, and turn the running end and pass it upwards through the loop until a second loop of the size required

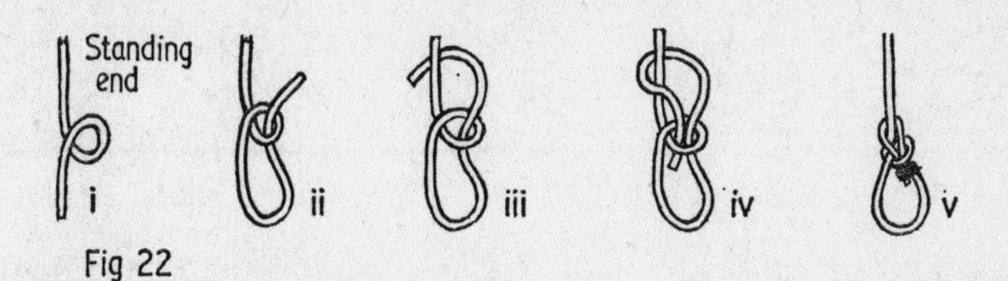

Fig 22

for the eye remains (ii). Pass the running end behind the standing part (iii), then downwards through the original loop (iv), and pull tight. Cut off what was the running end to about an inch, and for a permanent eye seize it to the side of the loop to keep it out of the way (v).

Deck Fittings

Fig 23 shows some fittings which you are likely to have in one form or another. The fairlead is used either to lead a rope from a cleat via a more suitable point for a particular purpose, or to prevent an anchor cable from chafing the hull. The decorative type of cleat often fitted to small runabouts is often pretty useless, too small for the job or so streamlined that lines slip off. Eye fittings are to keep main cleats free of fender lanyards; alternatively small cleats for this would also provide useful points for tying springs. To attach a line to a single stemmed cleat, samson post or single bollard, open out the eye, pull a bight (loop) of the line through it

Fig 23

(Fig 24 (i)), twist the eye so that it lays sweetly (ii), place the bight round the stem of the fitting and pull tight (iii). Alternatively, place the eye itself over the cleat then make a round turn with

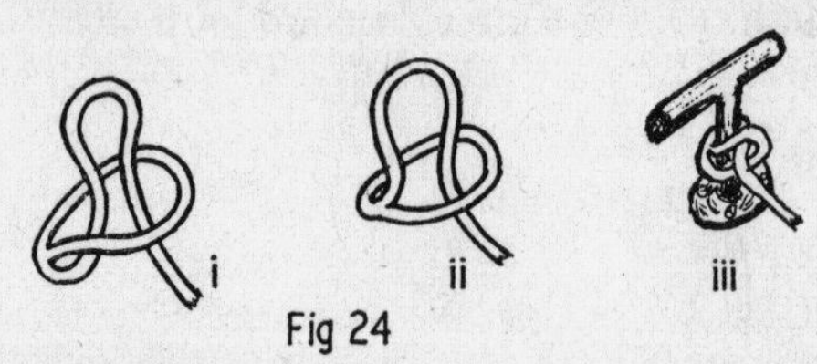

Fig 24

one side of the eye to prevent its coming off (Fig 25). On double stemmed cleats and double bollards, push the eye between the stems then turn it back over the entire fitting (Fig 26). All of these methods are secure and leave the top part of the fitting clear for tying off.

Fig 25 Fig 26

Make sure that all your lines are neatly coiled at all times, as you might need them unexpectedly. Many people get into difficulties when a line is not properly coiled before it is actually required (sometimes not even then). Time may be wasted in an emergency, as it may fall short when thrown, and have to be re-coiled. It is easy to trip over lines lying jumbled on the deck, or to catch the fingers while trying to unravel it and pull it at the same time. Untidy lines are worse than useless: they are positively dangerous.

THROWING A ROPE

Only throw a rope to someone ashore or on another boat whom you consider to be competent to handle it once caught. Stand close to the cleat to which it is attached, and pick up the rope in your best throwing hand. If there is any doubt about the tidiness of the coil, drop it and re-coil it. Hold it with the standing end leaving the top of the coil towards the cleat. With the other hand, remove a couple of turns from the standing end of the coil and drop them to give plenty of slack. Then, THROW THE WHOLE COIL, aiming at the recipient's chest. It is pointless throwing it to the ground somewhere nearby, because it will probably slide into the water before he can get to it. If it is thrown too high he will be more concerned with shielding his face (or saving his hat in the case of a lock-keeper) than with catching it. Throw neither over-arm, which causes the coil to collapse and knit itself, nor under-arm, which is likely to send it straight up in the air; but use a wide horizontal swing. Having thrown it, leave it alone: let the person ashore pull or pass it round a bollard and throw the remainder back to you for attention.

Do not throw lines ashore when there is nobody there to deal with them. If you are going ashore to deal with your own lines, take them with you, so that you are ready to pull the moment you land, and there is no risk of the unattended line slipping into the water out of your reach.

Even more useful is the ability to throw the centre of a line over a bollard whilst keeping the ends aboard the boat. With a 30ft line, it is possible in this way to reach a bollard over 12ft away. Longer, heavier lines will reach even further, though a very light line has insufficient weight to travel far.

Face the bollard selected, and whether you are left- or right-handed you must pick up the line in the hand nearest the cleat, with the standing end leaving the top of the coil towards the cleat. Drop a couple of turns from the coil at the standing end, and with the other hand drop a couple from the running end and hold the end. You should now be standing as in Plate eight. Without changing hands or fiddling with the line in any way, throw the rest of the coil hard enough to travel over and beyond the bollard so that it falls to the ground behind it. Any excess line beyond the bollard can quickly be pulled back aboard from the *running* end. Never pull in the standing end, as this will leave you holding both ends, with you and not the boat attached to the bollard. Should the boat move unexpectedly, you could be pulled over the side. Always handle the running end only, so that there is friction on the bollard and double the holding strength.

When using lines as an aid to stopping, always use the STERN LINE FIRST. Whether you are handling it from aboard or ashore, take a turn on the bollard and gently slow the boat to a stop. The line must be attached on the side you are coming in, to swing the boat in towards the landing. Do not stop her too hard, and never tie off solid until the boat has stopped, because this will slam her against the landing and could break the line or the cleat. If the rope slips uncontrollably round the bollard, take another turn or two, which will squeeze the bollard and act as an efficient brake which can be applied either gently to slow and stop the boat, or hard to hold her still.

Never use the forward line to stop a boat, as to do so causes the bows to hit the bank and the stern to swing out (see Plate seven).

Having thrown your lines over bollards from aboard, any extra turns will also have to be thrown, which is a very simple trick. A movement at one end of a line can be transmitted to the other, as shown in Fig 27. The point marked 'x' must travel to the left, upwards and away from you, falling beyond the bollard. So, with the line fairly taut, the hand must quickly describe a large circle: left, upwards and away, right and down. The resultant loop will run the length of the line until 'tripped' by the bollard, when it will fall over it and can be pulled tight. Pulling tight too soon, before the loop has time to fall, will pull it out straight and the

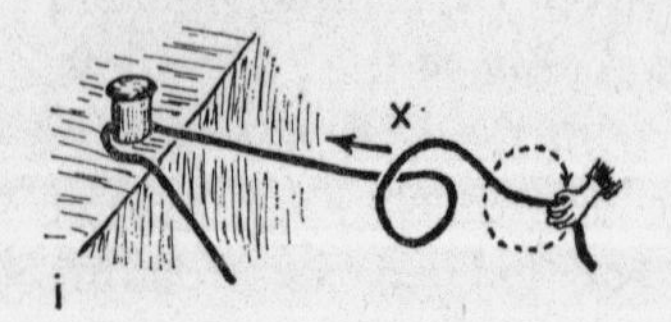

Fig 27

throw will be spoilt, but a little advance practice will enable you to throw turn after turn on and off bollards with complete confidence.

The bollards with horizontal pins through the body, used extensively on the Thames, require a much harder throw and a larger loop to clear the pin. These were introduced to prevent the lines of high-sided craft from slipping off, though if a bollard is used properly, with a round turn pulled tight and tended, this does not happen anyway. So the pins, fitted to help the less proficient, can not only make the bollards more difficult to use properly, but also cause lines to become jammed, often as a result of mis-use by taking a convenient clove hitch round the pin.

TYING UP

The technique of placing lines was discussed in Chapter five, and here we consider the knots or hitches to use. Surprisingly few will satisfy all your requirements; indeed professionals working with heavy lines on large craft rarely use a knot at all for mooring, as a heavy rope which pulls tight can be impossible to untie.

Using a Cleat

If the mooring point ashore is close enough, be it bollard, peg, tree, ring, or whatever, it is usually best to put a round turn on it and run the line back to the boat for tying off. This doubles the strength, keeps unused line out of the way of walkers and vandals who might feel compelled to untie it, and provides an easier place for tying off. The correct way is to pass the line once round the stem of the cleat, to take the strain, up and back over the centre, down under the other end, up again and across the centre in the opposite direction, and so on. Three or four turns on each end of the cleat will prevent the line from slipping off, but to finish off, form a loop with the running part under the standing part as in Fig 28, place it over the end of the cleat, and pull tight. There *must* be several turns on the cleat before taking this single half hitch, otherwise it could pull too tight to undo; and if the cleat is too small for several turns, finish off with a slipped half hitch (Fig 29), which is formed by using a bight of rope instead of the single length, and can be broken by pulling on the running end.

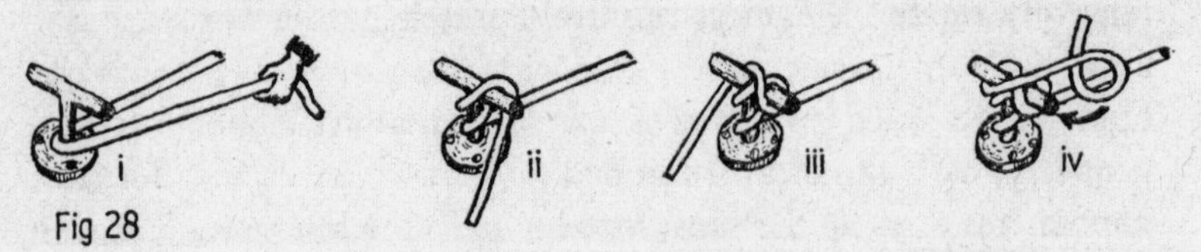

Fig 28

This method also applies when using little double bollards, which are practically the same in function as a cleat, though here it is often difficult to persuade half hitches to hold without using several on alternate sides of the fitting. It would be better, particularly if the line is a little small for the fitting, to use a Bargee's Hitch on only one bollard (see Plate eleven).

Half Hitches

These are probably the most useful of all knots and hitches. Most people use them all the time for tying almost anything, without even considering that they have a name other than 'knot' (which as it happens is wrong). Half hitches, as the name suggests, only form a complete hitch when used in pairs, though they are often used singly as above to finish other work. First take a round turn on the mooring point, and pass the running end over the standing part, underneath, and up through the loop thus formed. Then it goes down and under the standing part in the opposite direction to the previous hitch, up over the top and down through the second loop thus formed (Fig 30).

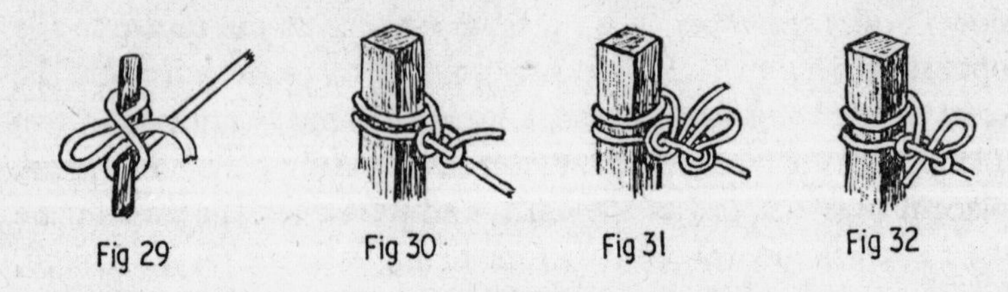
Fig 29 Fig 30 Fig 31 Fig 32

Plate 15 (above) Twin screws, separated by a deep keel and rudder, improve the power and handling of this Dunkirk veteran, but are of limited use inland;
Plate 16 (below) The revolutionary forward-facing propeller and streamlined gearcase and rudder on this new Aquafibre 44ft 10 berth John Bushnell hire cruiser are designed to improve handling

Plate 17 (*above*) These warning boards, displayed on Thames locks when the current becomes dangerous, are the signal for the prudent to check engines and anchors and don lifejackets. Hire firms mostly prohibit their craft from moving at such times;
Plate 18 (*below*) A 300-ton cargo boat dwarfed by Victoria Locks, Goole. The Ouse tideway beyond, connecting several waterways, should only be used by reliable and sufficiently powerful craft

If there is much spare line, do not pass the entire running end round and through each time, but simply double back a long bight in the line and make your hitch with that (Fig 31). If the line is subjected to great strain, half hitches can pull very tight, so to prevent this, take several round turns before tying off, or use a slipped half hitch for the second of the two (Fig 32). A variation is to use the slipped hitch first, to take the strain, and use the bight of this for the second hitch, to prevent accidental release.

Clove Hitch

You will remember that the second half hitch is formed in the opposite direction to the first. If it were formed in the same direction, the result would be a clove hitch. This is not suitable for tying a line to itself or to another line as it can pull extremely tight. However, it is quite useful for making fast quickly to a bollard, and has the same effect as two round turns, squeezing the bollard and preventing itself from running round, without the necessity of holding the end.

The easiest way to make a clove hitch is to twist the line into a bight with the standing part uppermost, and place this on the bollard (Fig 33 (i–ii)). Then make another bight the same, and place this on the bollard above the first (iii–iv), and pull tight. This hitch is very quick to tie, and therefore useful in an emergency,

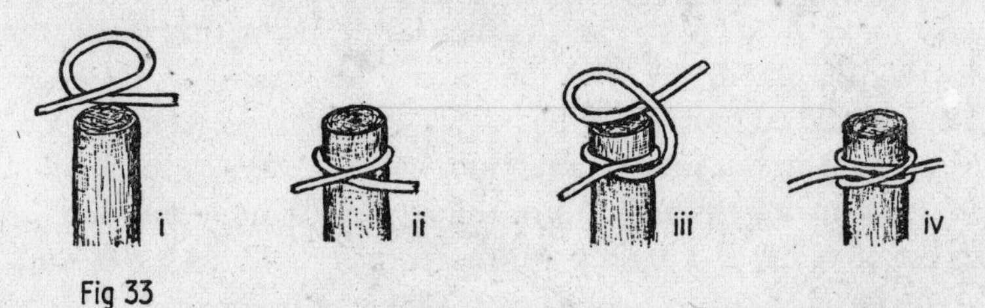

Fig 33

and with practice it is even quicker to pre-form the whole hitch and drop it complete on the bollard. Make the first bight as before, and hold it in the thumb and finger of one hand whilst forming the second with the other hand. Turn the two bights towards each other with the second above the first (Fig 34) and place them on the bollard, pulling tight as before.

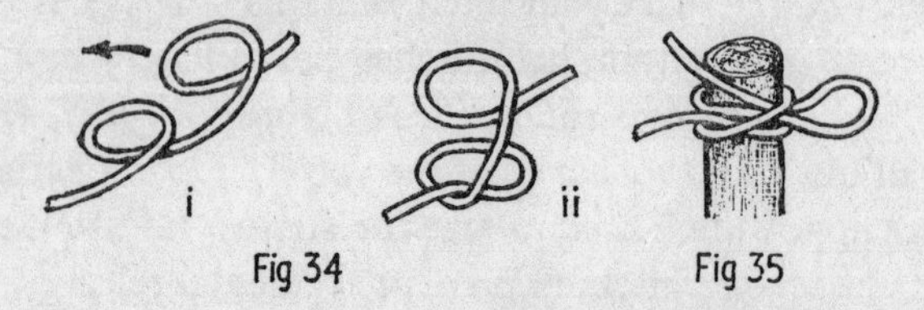

Fig 34 Fig 35

A clove hitch subjected to a heavy strain pulls very tight, and the slipped version (Fig 35) would be safer here. Equally, to avoid slipping, the hitch should be on the opposite side of the bollard to the strain.

Bargee's Hitch

Finally, there is a very effective way of using a bollard or mooring post, which is standard practice with heavy lines, but usually overlooked when using smaller ones. It is the easiest of all methods both to set and to remove: it cannot slip, cannot pull tight, and does not involve a single knot. Strangely, there does not seem to be a common name, so 'bargee's hitch' has been chosen out of respect for the professionals who use it all the time.

After passing the line round the bollard, with or without a round turn as you wish (Fig 36 (i)), pull a bight of the running end under the standing part (ii), then lift the bight, turn it towards the bollard and drop it over the bollard (iii). Pull tight, then pass the running end round the bollard as well (iv). This is unlikely to slip even without further attention, but it is usual to make quite sure by pulling through another bight as at (ii) and repeating the process. Now, it certainly will not slip, but to keep the work

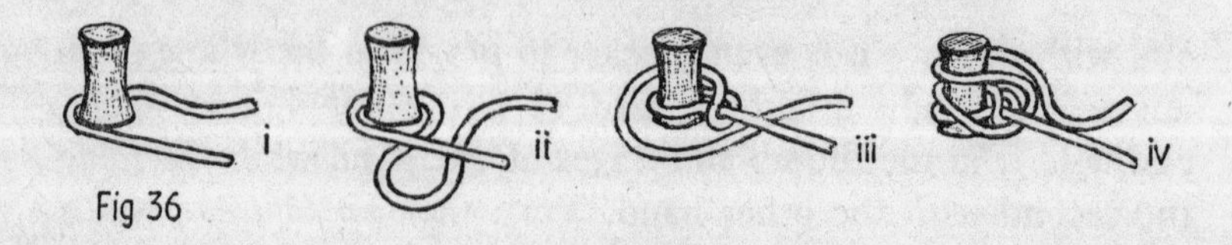

Fig 36

taut it is best finished off with a single half hitch either round the standing part of the line or on the bollard. As already mentioned, this hitch can also be used on a cleat, provided the stem is tall enough, and it is particularly suitable for use in anchor chain, which must never be knotted.

Although the hitches mentioned will satisfy most day-to-day requirements for inland boating, this is not to say that they constitute anything like a complete list. Knotting and splicing together form a fascinating subject for study, and there are several books available on the subject for those interested in pursuing it further.

CHAPTER SEVEN

LOCKS AND WEIRS

Rivers rise in high ground and flow down eventually to sea level, either directly or by joining one another. In its natural state, a river is in places too shallow for navigation, passing over rapids or natural waterfalls to lower reaches. As man learned to harness water power to drive machinery, many weirs were built across rivers to hold back the water so that it could turn water wheels as it fell from the higher level to the lower. On large rivers, this had the incidental effect of providing a reach of deep water which could be used by local barge traffic to transport produce between farms, mills, packhorse roads and any riverside towns and villages, and some weirs were built only for this purpose. Still more were built to trap fish or eels, which was a thriving industry in the British Isles two hundred years ago.

As the trade of an area developed, it became expedient to arrange for some means of allowing barges to pass these weirs. Originally this was done simply by opening a section of the weir and allowing the barge to pass through with the current or, if going upstream, it would be hauled through by a rope from a big capstan winch on the bank. This operation caused a 'flash' of water to be released, giving the name 'flash weir' or 'flash lock'. The flash would then travel downstream, helping the barges over shallows; but the process was very lengthy, extremely wasteful of water, and highly dangerous where the fall was greater than a couple of feet. On steeper gradients, flash weirs were therefore numerous, and it is not surprising that on the ancient river navigations these were replaced by the type of lock which is common today.

The 'pound lock', as this is called, is of doubtful origin, though the Chinese are said to have used them two thousand years ago. Early English ones, a mere three hundred or so years ago, were often nothing better than two flash weirs built close together. The short reach or 'pound' between them filled or emptied as the weirs above or below were opened, and the barges floating in the pound were transferred from one level to the other without much wastage of water. Over the years, the weirs at either end have been replaced by gates, with separate sluices for filling and emptying; though the only other changes in two thousand years have been the mechanical means of opening sluices and gates, and these vary from waterway to waterway and sometimes even from lock to lock.

Should you wish to delve into the history of locks or waterways in general, there are many books in the David & Charles list devoted to the subject in varying detail.

On canals, which are artificial waterways built especially for barges and boats, there are often large numbers of locks by which the canals climb up and down hillsides to serve areas out of reach of a navigable river. Most canals in Great Britain, constructed largely by private enterprise, were built with severe financial restrictions, often where the supply of water to fill them was none too plentiful. In England, locks were usually therefore limited to either 14ft or 7ft wide, and up to 72ft in usable length. Canal craft exactly fitted them. On steep gradients, the locks are often close together, sometimes within a hundred yards or so of one another, and this arrangement is call a 'flight'. On the steepest slopes, they are arranged so that one opens directly into the next, the upper (head) gates of one being also the lower (tail) gates of the next. Two locks connected in this way are called a 'double lock', or 'staircase pair', and three or more are referred to as a 'staircase' or 'three- (or other number) rise'.

A lock, then, is a very simple device, and works on a combination of gravity, manpower and water pressure, plus occasionally a touch of electrical or hydraulic power. After craft proceeding downstream have entered, the head gates are closed behind them and the water in the lock is emptied into the reach below through sluices at the tail. When the water level in the lock has dropped to match that below the water stops flowing and the gail gates, no longer held shut by the pressure of water in the lock, can then be opened. The boats then go out, and any craft proceeding upstream can enter. Now the tail gates are shut and their sluices closed, so that the level in the lock can be raised by filling from the reach above through the head sluices. Again, when the levels inside and outside equalise, the gates can be opened. Because the lock chamber holds a comparatively small quantity of water, the filling and emptying make little or no impression on the reaches above and below.

The sluices, which are situated either near the bottom of the gates or in culverts in the walls or floor of the lock, consist of apertures covered by vertically sliding doors of wood or steel called 'paddles', attached to rods which allow them to be operated from ground level. On most canals the rods are in turn attached to racks, which are raised by pinions on shafts which you wind with a cranked handle called a 'windlass' (pronounced as in 'bin'). On the Thames above Oxford, with its larger, heavier sluices, the system is counterweighted to make the operation easier, and you turn a spoked wheel instead of a windlass; while on the rest of the Thames the work is done hydraulically. On the River Nene, the tail gates are of the guillotine type, and are virtually just a single large sluice. The lock empties as you wind it up, but you have to take it right up overhead to let your boat out underneath. The 1¼in windlass is not available from the water authority, but the usual canal windlass will fit. However, on the Great Ouse, *only* the authority's own windlass or 'lock handle' may be used. These are available on hire and all others are banned.

Lock gates, of wood or steel, are usually opened and closed by pushing on the 'balance beam' attached to the top and forming not only a lever for the purpose, but also a means of counterbalancing the weight of the gate for easy operation as well as technical reasons. Some locks are fitted with cables and winches to open the gates, or even hydraulic pistons and electric motors.

Except on busy or large waterways like the Trent and Thames, and at certain locks to tidal waters, most locks are operated by boat crews. British Waterways issue clear instructions with their licences on how to work their locks, and the method itself holds good for locks anywhere. On some waterways, you need special keys to unlock the winding gear, a necessary precaution against vandalism.

Thames Locks

The Thames is the most popular cruising waterway with locks, and therefore deserves fairly detailed attention. The locks are large, in good condition, and manned by lock keepers whose job it is to work them and to attend to the weirs and to maintain water levels. Though not really part of their job, they are usually also prepared to help the less competent with lines, particularly hired boats on their first day, but most feel that after the first few locks you should be able to handle your own boat and lines. When busy, it is a full time and exhausting job shepherding two or three hundred boats a day through the lock, without having to catch most of them and tie them up.

When you arrive at a Thames lock, unless the gates are open to you, tie up on the lay-by as near as possible to the lock without obstructing boats which may come out, and wait. Do not tie up to floating booms or breakwaters, near which there is frequently a strong cross-current. When going downstream, remember that if the lock is already filling as you approach (which you can see by observing whether the hydraulic pistons on the gates are up, or the *red* marker on the winding gear of a hand-operated lock), the water may flow past your boat quite fast. Come alongside the lay-by as near parallel as possible and put the *stern* line out first to avoid being swung round. The same applies wherever there is a strong tail stream or tail wind.

If you do make a mistake, and swing round helplessly on the

bow line, the situation can be saved as in Chapter five (Fig 8) by using the engine to pivot the boat on its bows or bow line.

Even when the lock keeper opens the gates, wait for his signal before entering unless you can see that there are no boats to come out. Watch out for this signal so as not to waste valuable time in packing the lock, and acknowledge that you have seen it so that the lock keeper can turn his attention to the next boat. On a busy day, he may call boats in a particular order so as not to waste space, and it is not easy to communicate with a specific boat at two hundred yards range if crews are not paying attention. The usual method is to look or point directly at a boat, then give a beckoning signal and an indication of which side of the lock to go. A boat which will not fit may receive a 'halt' signal from one hand whilst a smaller one receives a beckon from the other.

Follow these instructions promptly. The lock keeper knows both his lock and the sizes of most boats, and can judge the operation to inches. Drive in just fast enough to steer straight to the appointed side. Keep in gear rather than drifting except for the last few feet, then stop by going astern. If it is busy, move right up the lock close to the gates or to the boat ahead, but if you are almost alone keep away from the head gates when going up because of the 'boil' from the sluices.

Unless directed otherwise, it is usually best to go to the side opposite to the boat ahead, even if that means changing lines and fenders to that side, as a vessel behind you may be too wide to pass you, and the space be wasted (as in Plate twelve) and someone else 'locked out' unnecessarily. Although it is the lock keeper's job to work out how to fit everybody into his lock, it is a great help if you understand what he is trying to do, and are ready and competent to act quickly on his instructions.

If you find yourself going too fast and are obliged to stop yourself with a line, USE THE STERN LINE from a fitting on the side on which you are coming in. (See page 84.) Plate seven shows the results of stopping a moving boat on the headline.

If it looks as though you are about to hit something hard, do not attempt to fend off with hands or feet unless you can do so above deck level. Serious injuries are caused by attempting to stop several tons of boat that way, but damage to the boat can be repaired.

Thames locks are well provided with bollards, but it is frequently necessary to hold your boat in a position for which they are not ideally placed and intelligent use of lines, working ahead and astern, is essential. Study again Figs 10, 11, 12 and 14 on mooring, but remember that in a lock you do not tie up. Pass your lines once round the bollards and back to the boat then hold the ends and adjust them to allow for the rise and fall of the water.

Once the boat is made fast, switch off the engine. This requirement is a fire precaution, and avoids filling the lock with fumes which are unpleasant to others, particularly those in small craft. It is also a requirement on the Thames that radios, cassette recorders, televisions and other noise-making devices are not played in a lock. They may prevent the lock keeper's instructions from being heard, perhaps in emergency; and three or four sets all blaring different programmes can make a most unpleasant din. In fact, wherever you are on the waterways (or elsewhere for that matter) do keep radios turned down so that they do not disturb others. Surprising though some seem to find it, not everybody shares one's own taste in entertainment, and the vast majority take boating holidays to get away from such things.

If you are near the head gates in a filling lock, there will be a certain amount of turbulence and a surprising tendency for your boat to be drawn *towards* the gates. This is because the water, entering under pressure through sluices at the bottom of the gates, literally bounces off the water already in the lock, as shown in Fig 37. Some of it rises and eddies towards the gates before being drawn downwards to circulate again. You must have a line working astern to prevent the boat from moving uncontrollably ahead. Have a turn on a bollard and somebody strong on the

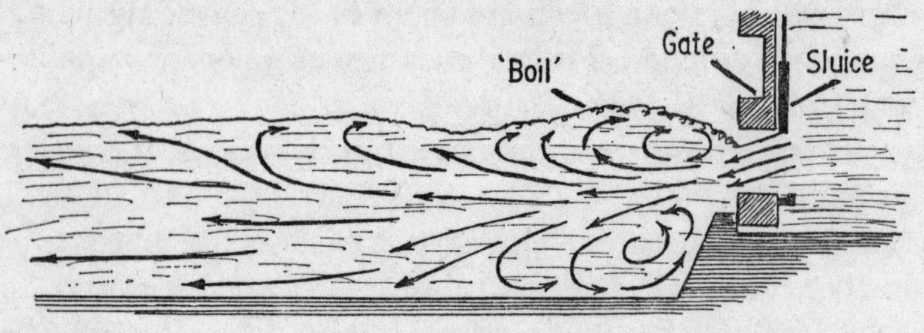

Fig 37

end: this is not a job for lightweight wives and children unless used to it.

Having set this line, usually from the stern, LEAVE IT ON THE BOLLARD. If it slips, take another turn, or snub it down to a cleat on the boat, but *never* take it off in the belief that you can control it better by a direct pull. Even a twenty footer can weigh well over a ton! Even if you have to take in some slack, keep this precautionary turn in case she takes a run.

When you have to share a bollard with the boat ahead, pass your line underneath theirs, since they will want to let go first. Watch that neither line traps the other on the pin of the bollard. In Fig 38, the smaller line was on the bollard first, with the lock at low level, and the second, larger line was dutifully passed underneath. But as the water rose, this came up outside the other, trapping it and making it difficult to adjust.

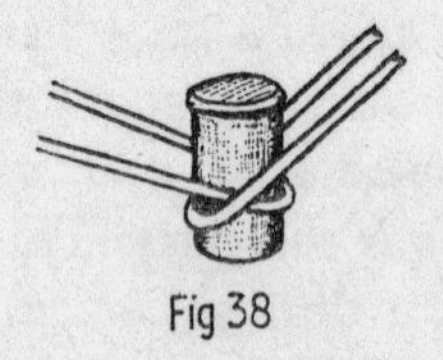
Fig 38

Equally, make sure that the running end of the line remains uppermost at all times. Never pull the boat in with the standing part of the line or place this as a round turn over the running end already on the bollard. On a falling lock, the result of this will be as in Plate ten, where the standing end has trapped the running end and prevented it from slipping round the bollard. The turn pulls ever tighter until the boat becomes hung up, and often the only way to free it is to refill the lock or cut the line. It is also easy to get the running end trapped under the pin as the lock fills. To avoid this, arrange the first turn below the pin and the whole round turn above.

When descending, check that the boat does not overhang the lockside, which can also cause a hang-up. Ensure that there is room to push her out, particularly if opposite a wide boat which may have similar problems the other side, and if necessary one or other of you must move a little ahead or astern before the lock starts emptying. This cannot happen on a rising lock, but look out for broken masonry and gate beamwork which could catch the boat. This too can be embarrassing, and crockery sliding off the shelves makes matters sound worse. Even if the lock keeper notices your trouble at once, the lock cannot instantly be reversed; nevertheless it is usually safer to wait for this than to try pushing or lifting the boat clear.

Since the water leaves the lock via the sluices in the tail gates, the turbulence when descending will be outside the gates and will not disturb those in the lock. (However, a craft too close to the gates outside the lock may be disturbed if not tended properly.) Descending is a quiet procedure, and it is not necessary to have more than a single turn on the bollards, though near the tail there can be quite a current past your boat.

Whichever way you are going, remain made fast until the gates are open and any craft ahead of you are moving, otherwise you will float about out of control and possibly cause damage. When ready to go, start the engine, let go the lines, push off a little and drive out in your turn and in single file. Don't overtake any powered boat until clear of the narrow lock cut, and don't forget to thank the lock staff. This small courtesy is too often forgotten even after they have spent time in helping and advising.

Thames locks are manned from 9am to a reasonable time in the evening varying from 5pm in winter to 7.30pm in summer. Most are manned all day in summer, though in winter and at odd times in summer a lock without an assistant will be unmanned for an hour's lunch and half-an-hour's tea break. The exact timing of these breaks is flexible, so that the lock keeper can go off duty at a time convenient to the working of the lock, instead of stopping dead on a certain time with a lockful of boats. However, if traffic is continuous, the poor man must at some time draw the line and stop for his meal, so please do not be one of the 'just lock us through first' brigade.

Operation of Locks by Boats' Crews

Outside working hours, including meal breaks, Thames locks may be operated by boats' crews, but the power equipment is not available to them. Full instructions are posted at the locks concerned, so there is no point in covering this here. The sluices of manual locks are operated by fixed handwheels on the gates. When a sluice is closed, a white marker protrudes from the top of the gear casing, and as you draw the sluice this is lowered and a red marker rises. You turn the wheel towards the marker you want to rise.

A couple of points need emphasising. As most locks leak, the tail sluices are usually left slightly drawn to keep them empty, and must be closed before the lock will fill. Always leave the lock empty after you with the gates closed both ends (there are often footpaths across them) and the tail sluices partly open if that was how you found them.

Canal and Other Locks

On the Trent, which is under the control of British Waterways, you leave the gates open as you go out, in either direction, if the lock keeper is not there. The four mechanical locks cannot be operated at all after hours, but 6am till 10pm should be long enough for anyone. On the Nene, you must leave the lock with the tail guillotine gate fully raised, so that if the water rises it can run away, and on all Fenland rivers all gates and sluices must be left as you found them, even if running water, as they are used for water level control, but on most canals you should close all paddles and gates to minimise water loss through leakage.

In fact, canal locks are a different story altogether from the busy Thames ones. Apart from their small size, they are mostly unmanned, and to operate them yourself you will need a windlass, which can be purchased from British Waterways or the relevant navigation authority, or from certain boatyards. Carry at least two, so that two people can share the work, making it quicker and easier, and to have a spare in case one is dropped in the canal. Although the mechanical devices by which the lock is operated vary, the method of working a lock described on pages 93–4 does not.

In *Holiday Cruising on Inland Waterways* the working of canal locks was covered in great detail, and you should acquaint yourself with the process before using the waterways. It is vitally important that water is not wasted by the avoidable misuse of locks, which even on the Thames can seriously upset the finely-adjusted levels.

Many canals suffer today, as they did when heavily used by commercial traffic, from the lack of an adequate supply of water to the highest level (summit). Every time a lock is worked, a lockful of water passes down to the pound below, and in times of drought some pounds can become very depleted. A stage is reached when the canal simply has to be closed until it or its reservoirs fill again naturally. One device on canals with this problem is the side pond built beside some locks. If there is a serviceable side pond, you must use it, as it saves about a third of a lockful of water with each operation.

The side pond is connected to the lock chamber by a culvert with a sluice. When the lock is full, instead of emptying it through the tail sluices into the next pound, you draw the sluice to the side pond. The lock empties into the pond until the levels are equal, with the lock half empty. You now close the side paddle, and discharge the rest of the lockful into the pound below, via the tail paddles. To fill the lock, the side paddle is drawn first with all the other paddles closed, and (the water from the side pond runs back into the lock until the levels are equal, when again the side paddle is closed and the remainder of the filling done via the head paddles in the usual way. Some locks have two side ponds at different levels, together saving about half a lockful of water each time.

On arrival at a canal lock, land a party to work it. Treat the (often rickety) gates with care: don't try to open them before the levels are correct, nor push them with the boat in case there is a log trapped behind them. Slamming the gates by drawing the paddles before they are closed can cause serious damage. To put a narrow boat into a 7ft lock, the boat must first be straightened if necessary, by placing the bows GENTLY into the opening, putting the tiller hard over and going full ahead to kick the stern round into line. Rubbing the walls or gates gently will not hurt them: hitting them hard at an angle will. In the lock, use the engine to hold the boat clear of gates or sill, keeping closer to the tail if ascending. On leaving, wait in the opening whilst the lock party closes the gates behind you.

WEIRS

Since most land drainage is done by the natural river system, a canal rarely receives water in larger quantities than it can cope with, and any weir is usually only a small overspill to carry away any excess water caused by working the locks.

A river, whether small or large, must be able to pass its normal floodwater without bursting its banks, and on the Thames, this is done by having adjustable weirs which are operated by the lock keepers. A constant watch is kept on the water levels and on rain gauges throughout the catchment area, and all lock keepers are informed by their colleagues upstream, as well as by a central information room, of any factors likely to upset the levels. The weirs are then adjusted accordingly. In contrast, on the recently restored upper (Stratford) Avon, to avoid the expense of manning weirs, solid wide overspill weirs were built. The disadvantage of these is that they cannot pass an increased volume of water until the level above them rises appreciably, and the river rises and falls abruptly after heavy rainfall, which must be allowed for when mooring.

The weirs on the Trent are also mainly of this type, except the enormous Holme sluice below Nottingham, which keeps the level fairly constant for the city. The river banks are built up high or reinforced to cope with large rises in level.

It is worthwhile considering how a weir is likely to affect your progress. Weirs are often placed at an angle across the river, to give a wider overfall than would otherwise be possible. (In the days of flash weirs, this also meant that a winch on the bank could pull the barges upstream in a straight line.) Such a weir near the head of a lock requires the greatest care when tackle is drawn, for the natural flow of the river is towards the weir and not towards the lock. There is no danger provided you keep away.

When the weir is at the tail end or angled in the opposite direction, there is little danger of going too close from above, but the back-eddy at the tail of the lock can have a considerable effect on a boat. In the example in Fig 39, when the stream is fairly strong you should approach when going upstream in the slacker water on the inside of the bend (A). You will have to cross the faster water to reach the lock, which is on the left (B). As you do

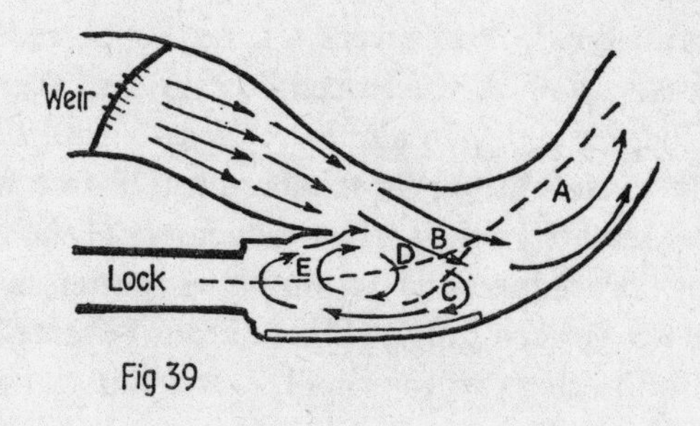

Fig 39

so, put the helm a little to the right, crossing slightly crabwise to avoid being swept across to the left bank (C). On leaving the fast water, the bows enter the eddy (D), and will be pushed to port. You have to correct this by steering slightly to starboard, but by the time the stern is under the influence of the eddy, the bows will be pushed to starboard by the far side of it (E), and quite heavy action with the helm will be necessary to prevent this.

As a last gesture of defiance, the eddy at (E) gives your stern one final shove to starboard, twisting the boat to port, which again must be corrected by steering to starboard before straightening and slowing down to enter the lock. Do not slow down earlier, as this will leave you longer in the eddy with less way to correct the steering. The golden rule is that if the boat is not going fast enough to respond quickly to the helm, *increase engine speed* at once until the helm takes over again. *Then* slow down, perhaps using short bursts of power to manoeuvre.

Often, a weir is well away from a lock, and the disturbing effect as you pass the outlet of the weirstream can be unexpected unless you are following a map. The only danger is of being swept sideways into the bank or the path of other craft; but where you pass above an unexpected weir, as on the Trent where the Newark Cut leaves the natural river as it tumbles over the vast Averham weir, the draw towards the overfall can be considerable. The two advance signs and row of marker posts along the overfall should give ample warning, and in general weirs and fast water are not dangerous provided that your boat is reliable and you know what you are doing.

When in full flood, most rivers are not to be recommended except for seasoned and experienced boaters, and there is advice to these in Chapter eight. In summer, cross-currents and eddies will normally cause little or no trouble on tide-free waters, and can usually be seen from the surface movement of the water. Like most boating procedures, it is simply a matter of *observing*, *thinking*, and *acting* accordingly; if conditions become hazardous, lock keepers and others will normally warn you.

CHAPTER EIGHT

ADVANCED BOATING

Inland boating is normally a leisurely and relaxing way of taking a holiday. It would hardly be so popular if it were one long chore from start to finish. You do not have to spend all your time worrying about dangers, nor does it really matter much if you never do learn to steer perfectly straight, although most regard it as part of the fun to become as proficient as possible. There is great satisfaction as well as comfort in knowing that your line will go over the bollard every time, and the boat always finish exactly where you intend.

As previously stated, several lovely cruising grounds are only accessible from other areas via a tideway. There are also advantages to cruising out of season, particularly on the Broads and Thames which are very busy on a summer's weekend; but there is then a greater risk of floods. Since most hire firms ban their craft from tidal or flooded waters, prospective hirers should check the position before booking their boat. An owner will have no such problem provided he is insured for 'inland and coastal waters of Great Britain' or similar wording (but be careful: some cheap policies specify a certain period laid-up in winter).

TIDEWAYS

A tideway is that part of a river affected by the tidal movement of the sea into which it flows. Tides are caused by the gravitational effect of the moon and, to a lesser extent, the sun, and as both of these and the earth revolve around each other in a perfectly regular and predictable rhythm, the movement of the tides is also predictable, taking about 12½ hours for a complete cycle.

Once every fifteen days, the sun and moon pull in the same direction, causing exaggerated 'spring' tides, and midway between these periods the smallest or 'neap' tides occur. The greater volumes of water flowing up and down a tideway during spring tides cause much swifter currents than on neaps, and both the tidal range and the current vary constantly between these extremes.

The limit to which average tides flow up a navigable river is the last lock and weir—Cromwell on the Trent, Naburn on the Yorkshire Ouse, Upper Lode, Tewkesbury on the Severn, Allington on the Medway and Teddington on the Thames. At Richmond, on the Thames tideway a few miles downstream of Teddington, there is a unique half-tide lock and weir, where the huge weir sluices are drawn right up into an overhead bridge until the tide is halfway out, then lowered into the water to hold back the rest and prevent the river at Richmond from drying out at low tide. Landwater coming down the river either spills over the top as on any other weir, or is allowed through a partially-open sluice. When the next tide reaches that level, they are again drawn, and in the meantime craft have to pass through the adjacent lock, the only one on the river operated by the Port of London Authority.

The natural flow of a river is reversed in the tideway as the rising tide flows up it from the sea. The upstream end of the tideway fills like a lake, augmented by landwater and by the funnelling effect of the narrowing channel, which combine to cause the tide to rise more rapidly than it ebbs. On the Trent, the tide at Trent Falls floods for about 4 hours, rising 10–16ft, and ebbs for about 8 hours, whilst 50-odd miles upstream at Cromwell Lock it only rises for about 1 hour, and then only 1–2ft.

Because the high water takes some time to travel these distances, by the time it reaches Cromwell it will already have been ebbing at Trent Falls for almost 4½ hours, so a boat working down with the tide will have less than 4 hours to reach the Ouse unless the skipper decides to tide-bash against the last of the flood at the beginning of the trip, or the first of the next flood at the end. The latter is best, and gives a good flood for working up the Ouse, though a low-powered boat might more easily stem the last of the previous flood, when the water is slacker.

Bores

When an incoming tide is impeded by a narrow or shallow reach, it can form quite an accumulation of water which then flows rapidly upstream. On certain rivers and at certain times (usually on spring tides and predictable), this accumulation rushes up the ever-narrowing channel as a wave, breaking at the edges, called a 'bore'. The celebrated Severn Bore is the best known, but the Trent and Ouse occasionally have a small one, called locally the 'Eagre' or 'Aegir'. Tidal information, which is a must for a successful tideway passage, will make it easy to avoid a bore, but it is possible to ride them head-on. It is not, however, either wise or necessary to hit a large Severn Bore (which can reach the alarming height of 6ft travelling at 10mph, below Gloucester), as it is avoided by using the Gloucester & Sharpness Canal.

Using the Tide

You will realise that some advance planning is necessary for successful negotiation of a tideway. If it forms part of a longer inland cruise, you need to select the most convenient tide and arrive in good time for it. As a deep-draught boat may be unable to use a particular tidal lock at low water, or not at all on neap tides, you must also know the range of the tide and the availability of the lock. The times of high water and the predicted heights at certain major ports are published in *Reed's Almanack* and some daily newspapers, and are available from harbour authorities and keepers of tidal locks. Figures for other points are calculated as a certain time before or after these 'Standard Ports' by reference to constants shown on charts and guides.

From this information, it is easy to work out the timing of your tideway trip, aiming for a time when: (i) the tide will be with you for as much of the trip as possible; (ii) there will be sufficient depth all the way, including tidal locks; and (iii) there will be sufficient headway under bridges.

In water moving at between 5 and 10mph, you could be travelling over the ground at nearly 20mph, and can cover surprising distances in a short time, whereas punching against the tide will take many times longer, and progress might be impossible. By starting upstream too early on a flood tide, you can actually overtake the flood and find yourself in slack or opposing water, though you cannot overtake an ebb, which turns first in the lower reaches.

Be sure where you intend to leave the tideway or to moor, as even in a modest 5mph tide the water in which you are floating travels 440ft in a minute, and you must take this into account and start turning before you reach the lock or mooring to avoid being swept past it.

Working against the Tide

Avoid tide-bashing if possible except for short periods for a particular purpose as above, as it is a waste of time and fuel. The engine has to be run at high speeds which, if unaccustomed, can cause excessive wear, overheating and possibly breakdown. With an engine used to high speeds in estuaries, skiing lakes or at sea, this will not apply.

With the best of planning, however, delays can occur, and if as a result you arrive late for your tide, you must choose whether to continue and risk the tide's turning before you reach you destination, or to wait for the next tide. If you decide on tide-bashing, seek the slowest water, which is on the insides of the bends, or towards the sides on a straight reach. Slow water is usually shallower, because that is where silt is deposited; on the other hand, a shoal may actually increase the speed of flow when the tide turns, because there is less room for the water to pass. Much of this can be read from the appearance of the foreshore, the banks, and the surface of the water itself. Swirling, flattish water is usually deep, whilst broken, choppy water is likely to be shallower unless obviously caused by the wind.

Remember that a craft running with the tide has right of way over you, and will want to cross from side to side to find the best of the tide just where you will be crossing to find slack water. If in doubt, use the appropriate navigation signal (Chapter nine). This does not give you right of way, but simply lets the other chap know what to expect, and he should give an opposite signal if your intentions would obstruct him.

Tideway Bridges

Bridges require special care in a strong stream, for the piers create a considerable wash, and also tend to hold back the water, sometimes giving an appreciable 'fall' under the arches. When proceeding with the tide, put your boat straight through the centre of the arch selected. This will normally be at or near the middle of the river, though if the bridge is on a bend or near an island or shoal, the deeper water may be towards the side. If it looks rough under the main arch, you may prefer the calmer side arches, but remember that craft punching against the tide will expect these to be clear for them, and that at low water there may be insufficient depth.

Your passage through the bridge may be bumpy. You will gather speed, and may have to increase engine speed to maintain steering control, emerging like an express from a tunnel. Do not try to slow down: speed will not hurt you, but loss of control might! A small boat will be pushed around by the complicated little currents at the obstruction, and you must use the helm quickly and hard to correct this. The usual rule applies: if she will not respond satisfactorily to the helm, use more helm and/or more revs.

A bridge on a bend can require more care, particularly in a long narrow canal boat, for even when your bows are comfortably in the centre of an arch, the stream still pushes sideways at the stern in an attempt to put it through the adjacent one! Approach the bridge obliquely from the inside of the bend so that this pushing will only straighten you, then turn quite hard as you leave the bridge in order to round the rest of the bend.

When negotiating a bridge against the tide, remember again that anything coming the other way has right of way for the very good reason that it could not possibly stop. You can: and must if necessary. Use an inside arch where there will be less likelihood of meeting anything. You may have to increase speed in order to climb up each wave under the bridge, so if you are already at full throttle and making little headway, it is safer not to attempt to pass the bridge but to anchor or moor and await slacker water.

An expert in a small and 'boat-shaped' boat can in fact use the wash from the bridge piers to help him through as follows. Enter the arch slightly to one side of its centre, to be in the wash of only one pier. If the boat fails to climb out of a trough, alter course very slightly towards the pier, travelling diagonally along the trough. When close enough to the pier for safety, alter course away from it and the boat will climb over one or more waves. Before reaching the rougher water at the centre of the arch, alter course towards the pier again and repeat the performance. As you climb over the last wave, head for a point beyond the centre of the arch, where the water will be slower than where it is building up around the piers, and make your best speed away from the bridge.

Be warned that this manoeuvre is dangerous if your boat is not fully reliable.

Tideway Hazards

Probably the greatest general danger on a tideway is from the large amount of driftwood which finds its way into the river as it passes a large town or industrial or dockland areas. This ranges from small pieces of wood to railway sleepers, pallets and doors. It can accumulate for some time before being swept out to sea because much of it is collected by a rising tide and carried further inland to be stranded as the tide falls. Flotsam is not always easy to see, particularly in choppy water, so watch closely for it.

At low water when much of the width of the channel may dry out, it is important to keep away from the banks, use the centre or other marked arches of bridges, and follow the course marked on the map or chart. Mud banks and islands must be avoided, and indeed can present a hazard at any state of the tide unless you know them well. On a tideway, shoals are not only found on the insides of bends, but may form elsewhere due to silt being brought up by the swift flood tide and deposited at slack water and on the slower ebb. A sandbank is unlikely to inflict serious damage to a boat, though to go aground on a falling tide can mean hours of delay before you refloat on the flood.

Drainage outlets laid in concrete well out into the centre may protrude above the bed due to erosion. Dangerous ones are usually marked, but keep well clear of any concrete groin disappearing into the water: you do not know how far it may extend.

On the Trent, training walls consisting of rocks spread down the banks are used extensively, and as these deteriorate the otherwise soft bed in the vicinity becomes strewn with boulders. Again, keep away.

Commercial Vessels

All navigable tideways in Britain are used by commercial craft, from the 60ft Humber keels to the tugs and strings of lighters of London; from the 500-ton cargo boats or push-tugs and lighters of the North East to the really large ocean-going ships found on them all. When empty, many of these craft draw only a few feet of water and operate at all states of the tide, often throwing up a gigantic wash as they punch the tide. They, like you, want the fastest water when running with the tide, and the slowest when going against, when they will go as close to the insides of bends as they dare. A cruiser going in the same direction at a slower speed will be overtaken, and although according to maritime practice the overtaking craft should give way and the overtaken one maintain its course and speed, some authorities require pleasure craft to give way to commercial craft under all circumstances; and in any case it is not comfortable to be caught on the inside of a narrow bend as a large ship overtakes you. The water is drawn away from the shallows and then thrown back there as breaking waves, and a small boat could be dropped quite hard on the bottom. If there is room, line up for the bend far enough out to clear the bottom, and the ship must either wait or take a still wider course. Otherwise, either round-up in good time before the ship catches up with you, meeting its wash head-on, then round-up again and follow it, or if clear pull over to the outside of the bend until the ship has passed.

When meeting other craft, commercial or otherwise, the one proceeding with the tide normally takes the outside of the bends and the other the inside. On straight reaches, the normal 'rule of the road' afloat applies (see Chapter nine).

RIVERS IN FLOOD

Flooding of a river is more likely in the cold winter months than in summer. Dormant vegetation drinks little or no water, whereas in summer it absorbs incredible quantities; and rainwater runs quickly off hard or saturated ground. Ditches and streams which in summer are clogged by rushes and weeds pass it rapidly into rivers, which suddenly rise.

However, floods sometimes occur in summer after prolonged rainfall, making boating difficult for beginners. Some rivers, like the Ancholme in Lincolnshire or the Northamptonshire Nene are used as land drains, and at such times traffic may be impossible. On the Thames, red warning boards are exhibited at locks when the weirs become dangerous, and this is the signal for hired craft to tie up on some mooring recommended by the lock keeper and contact the hire firm for permission to continue. In a private boat, it is your decision whether or not to proceed, and provided you are competent and alert, and your boat reliable, manoeuvrable and powerful enough, there is no reason why you should not.

A flooded river differs from a tideway in that you can only use the stream in one direction, and will have to punch against it on the return trip. The banks may be submerged in places. Trees and bushes may mark them, or they may not follow the banks at all, or there may be a submerged towpath. All the comments about fast tidal waters apply equally to fast rivers, but take extra care to avoid obstructions which would not normally be submerged: landing stages, piles, bridge pier projections, and so on. The headroom of bridges, not designed for these unusual conditions, will also be suspect.

Keep away from weirs, as already advised in Chapter seven. There is often a considerable draw towards them, and most are virtually unprotected, as booms or even piles and chains could seriously impede the flow. Be ready for strong cross-currents and eddies as a weir stream leaves and rejoins the navigation channel.

Mooring in Floods

Partially submerged banks are most inconvenient for mooring, as tree stumps, landing stages and other obstructions may be hidden beneath the surface off an otherwise inviting bank. The normal slow approach, sounding for depth with a shaft, is impossible, and you must keep her headed into the stream, slow down until stationary over the ground, and edge carefully sideways towards the mooring. Have the crew sounding at the *stern* to ensure that the propeller and rudder will not foul anything and that there is room to drop astern should the bows touch an obstruction.

Once alongside, tie up temporarily and have a really good feel around with the shaft or boathook. Check that you are not over a bank which will emerge if the level drops unexpectedly, or stakes which will hole the bottom of the boat. There may be safer depth a little further out, and if so moor as in Fig 40 with an anchor over the side to hold you away from the bank. The anchor is set well ahead, unlike the situation in Fig 15 (p 67), to hold you against the faster water and to prevent the boat from see-sawing on its lines. These should be set as long and as horizontal as possible so that a change in level does not affect the slackness too much. A gang-plank will probably be necessary here, and must be lashed to the boat to prevent its being dislodged by movement.

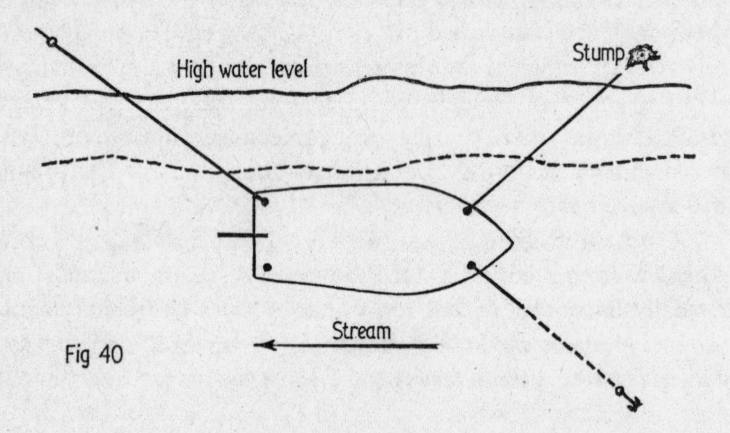

Fig 40

In these conditions, tie up if possible to trees or other solid points rather than relying on mooring pegs, which pull out of soft waterlogged ground. If spending the night on the mooring, check all lines for over-slackness or tightness before turning-in, and arrange for someone to wake during the night to check again.

When leaving the mooring, after starting the engine and warming it up, let go first the after line, then the head line and pull in any stern anchor (which should be alongside the boat). Finally, move ahead and take in the main anchor cable as in Chapter five.

Like a tideway, a river in flood carries driftwood plus the odd half-submerged dinghy, because logs, trees and boats often float off banks where they had been left. Flotsam lingers in the river for some while after the level has returned to normal, but after a few weeks most of it is stranded, or removed from weirs.

STEERING ASTERN

It takes most people all their time to keep straight when going ahead. To steer astern needs a fair amount of confidence, because you can only begin to steer at all when you have reached a fair speed. With an outdrive or outboard it is comparatively simple: point the propeller in the direction required, and the rest of the boat will more or less follow. If the bows swing around in the wind, turn the wheel to keep the propeller pointing in the right direction, and she will eventually straighten.

Not so with an inboard boat. Boats, propellers and rudders are not designed to go backwards, and most have to be cajoled into doing so. The reversed flow of water past the rudder tries to push it round to one side or the other, and it takes a firm hand on the helm to prevent this, particularly if the steering is slack. No sooner have you prevented a swing one way, than the rudder whips round the other way, the helm itself only following after the boat has begun to follow the rudder. But with luck, you might be able to set the helm against the paddlewheel effect of the propeller to keep straight.

Once the boat has gathered way, the hull has at least some tendency to keep straight, and steering becomes easier because slight wanders are perceptible before they have time to develop into lurches. So do not give up at the first sign of obstinacy by the boat.

'Who wants to go astern anyway, except to stop?' Well, there are many circumstances when it is either necessary, or at least easier than turning. For example, if somebody drops an expensive fender overboard while under way, it is quicker to stop and go astern to pick it up than to wait for a convenient gap in the traffic and go about. Or perhaps you are almost into a bridgehole from downstream when you realise that there are a tug and barges coming towards you. Or again, you have selected a cosy looking mooring for the night, only to go aground 20ft out. There is nothing for it but to reverse out, to where you know you have sufficient depth. When you have to reverse a boat, it must be done skilfully and accurately. The fact that you will rarely perform a manoeuvre does not mean that it is not worth practising—quite the opposite.

TOWING

Tenders

On a busy waterway, the best place for a tender is somewhere on board, out of the way. If you are compelled to tow it, the first essential is a good fender on its bows, for it will run forward and hit your stern every time you stop. Towing closely will prevent it from doing so too hard and largely eliminate the tendency to yaw from side to side. This can be prevented completely by using two tow ropes as a bridle from the quarters as in Fig 41 (upper sketch).

A tender is a nuisance in a busy lock, and it is often necessary to pull it round across the stern of your boat. For this reason, many people prefer to tow from just one quarter, with a slack line from the stern of the tender to the other quarter ready for pulling across if necessary. This is shown in Fig 41 (lower sketch).

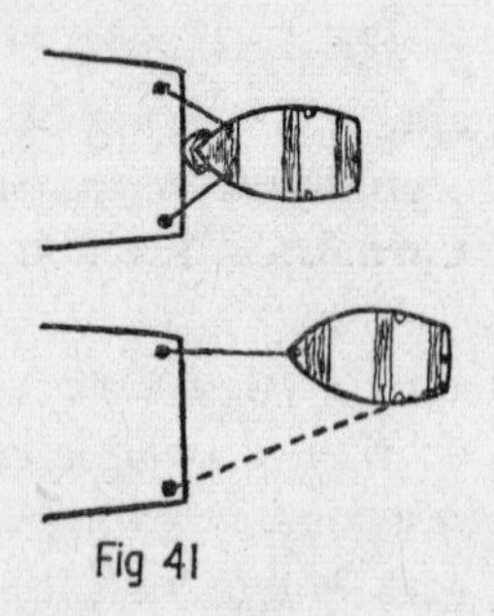

Fig 41

When using a busy public mooring, take your tender alongside the launch to leave more room for others; but to tow it in this position would be a nuisance in locks, as you cannot foretell to which side you will have to moor.

Larger Craft

Tow a disabled craft astern of you only if there is someone to steer it and to have lines ready to stop it. A tug normally tows from a post or hook amidships, so that even with a close tow its stern can swing in order to steer. This is why tugs have any superstructure built well forward. If as is probable, you do not have this arrangement, and have to tow from right aft, use a long line which will allow your stern to swing without sending the towed boat off in the opposite direction.

It is often better, and essential if there is nobody to steer the other boat, to tow alongside. Lash the two craft in such a way that they can ride up and down independently yet cannot move fore-and-aft. If the towing vessel is the smaller, it should be lashed as far aft as possible on the other, to improve steering. Incidentally, lightweight boats with outboards or outdrives are usually most unsuitable as tugs. Lash the helm of the towed vessel amidships or slightly *towards* the towing vessel to offset the tendency for the one propeller to push the whole lot round to the opposite side. On a twin-screw boat, it might help to use mainly the engine on the tow side.

In Fig 42 lines 'A' and 'D' hold the boats firmly together for ease of steering, while backspring 'B' takes the strain for towing and forespring 'C' for stopping. Additional lines would reinforce these and provide a safeguard in the event of one of the other lines snapping or cleats pulling from the deck under the unaccustomed strain.

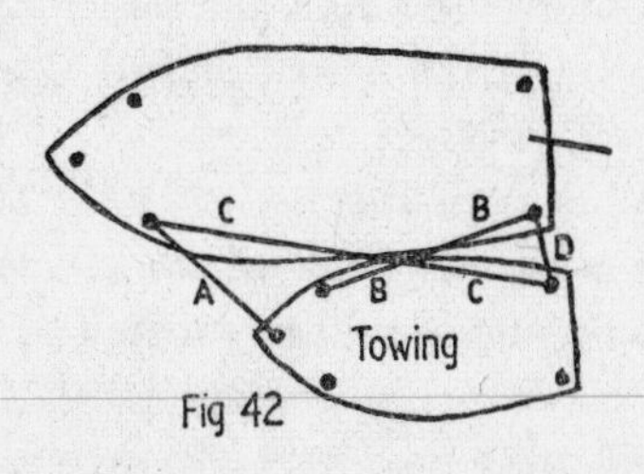

Fig 42

To start off you will need full rudder against the drag of the other boat, but once under way less corrective rudder will be needed. Stopping will be another matter, as the momentum of the towed boat will pull you round sideways if you go hard astern. Slow down well in advance and have plenty of fenders both sides as well as strong stern lines ready on whichever craft will be laid alongside (both if entering a lock). If you meet another craft, particularly one with right of way over you, give four blasts on the horn to indicate your inability to manoeuvre, or give a signal to indicate you intentions (see Chapter nine).

Other Objects

Large logs or waterlogged boats in midstream are a danger and should if possible be towed to the bank and tied up. Attaching a line from a high-freeboard cruiser may be difficult, and unless you can pass it round something substantial with the boathook, you may have to use the dinghy if you have one. Never get aboard a waterlogged boat. It may have insufficient buoyancy to support your weight, and will almost certainly capsize. At least you would get a ducking, and at worst could be trapped underneath.

With a log, unless there is a convenient branch it will be necessary to pass the line right underneath and take two turns to prevent its slipping off. If slipping cannot be prevented, tie the line round the thinnest part, or where there is a projection, then lead it to the end of the log and put a single hitch round the log before tying off aboard your boat. Always use slipped hitches, because half-submerged objects put a tremendous strain on them, and if possible tie so that the lines can be let-go from the boat in an emergency. Towing from a quarter will diminish any attempt for the tow to yaw. Tow a tree trunk-first or it will be completely uncontrollable. When you reach the bank, remove your lines and replace them with old ones which are useless for normal purposes but ideal for such a public-spirited act.

These and other eventualities occur rarely for most of us. If you are at home in your boat and competent to handle it, you should be able to apply your knowledge and experience to each new challenge as it appears. You never stop learning, practising, varying your techniques. Read as widely as possible about any intended cruising waters so that you know in advance what demands are likely to be made of you and the boat. If you are worried, reconnoitre by land first. This might well show that warnings of quicksands, wrecks, tidal races and other daunting prospects have been grossly exaggerated (though still deserving a healthy respect). Skill and confidence you may have, but you are no sailor if you neglect to find out what you are letting yourself in for and to be prepared. Only a fool believes he is so good that nothing can go wrong.

CHAPTER NINE

NAVIGATIONAL REQUIREMENTS

Although your first day or so afloat will be spent practising how to handle the boat, you must at the same time be aware of and observe the navigational rules and requirements of the waterway you are using. Some authorities require the crew of every boat to be 'adequate and competent', which is prefectly reasonable; and in the Humber and Trent and Ouse tideways this must consist of at least two people.

Course

The rule of the road afloat is generally that you keep to the centre of the channel except when meeting oncoming craft. Then you go to starboard (right) of them, passing 'port to port', when possible and expedient. All this contrasts sharply with British road practice, not only in passing on the right instead of the left but also in being extremely flexible, though under fairly well defined circumstances.

Keeping to the centre gives your wash further to travel before reaching the banks, thus reducing the erosion which any wash causes, however small; and also generally puts you in the deepest water except on a bend, where the deeper water is usually towards the outside. On a river, the current sweeping round the outside scours away material which is deposited as silt by the slacker water on the insides of bends. On a canal, as the stern of a long boat swings wide round a bend, its propeller churns up the mud which again is mainly deposited on the inside where the water is not thus disturbed. Therefore, keep slightly towards the outside of a bend if it is clear to do so. You will usually make better headway in deep water, and shallow water can slow you down and cause excessive wash.

On meeting another craft, both should normally alter course a little to starboard so as to pass port to port, but if for some reason the other deliberately alters course to port instead, you should follow suit to pass starboard to starboard instead. He may need deeper water, or be heading for a mooring or swinging wide to negotiate a bridge or a bend.

Navigation Channels

It is advisable to keep to the channel which is maintained and recommended for navigation. Backwaters leading to mills, weirs or behind islands are often shallow or weedy and sometimes private. It may be difficult or impossible to turn at the end. On a river, use a chart if available, though where it is important to follow a particular course, it is usually marked either with notices (especially on the Trent and the Warwickshire Avon) or with buoys (as on the Broads and Thames). On the tidal Trent, shoals are marked by white discs on poles on the nearest bank, though with the decline in commercial craft some of these are missing. Keep well clear, as there is no clue as to how far the shoals extend or at what state of the tide they are safely submerged. Further downstream and on the Ouse there are beacons which flash at night and are easily visible by day.

On the Thames, buoys with shaped and coloured topmarks are used, based on standard maritime practice, so let us consider briefly how the system works. The tides at sea, far from simply rising and falling as it appears from the beach, flow in certain directions around our coasts. Channel marker buoys follow an internationally recognised system of colours and shapes: when going with the *flood* (rising) tide, you leave buoys with body or topmark can-shaped, and/or coloured red, to port, and those with the shape of a cone or diamond and/or coloured black to starboard. The shapes or colours vary slightly, but always include one or more of the elements mentioned. Thus anything red, or red and white, or can-shaped is left to port, and anything black, or black and white, or even white, and/or conical, is left to starboard. Any buoys lit at night follow the system: leave red to port, white to starboard.

Since the system applies when travelling with the flood tide, and since the flood tide flows up river tideways *upstream*, any buoys on the non-tidal part of the river are also read as above when going upstream, *not* with the stream. When going downstream, or against the flood, or with the ebb, all buoys must of course be read in reverse.

A spherical shaped red and black buoy may be found on a midstream obstruction. Pass this on either side as circumstances dictate. Buoys marking wrecks are painted green, and again the can shape is left to port, cone or diamond to starboard and sphere to either side when going upstream. (Green flags or lights also denote a wreck.) Keep clear of all buoys, as the shoals they mark may extend well beyond the actual buoys.

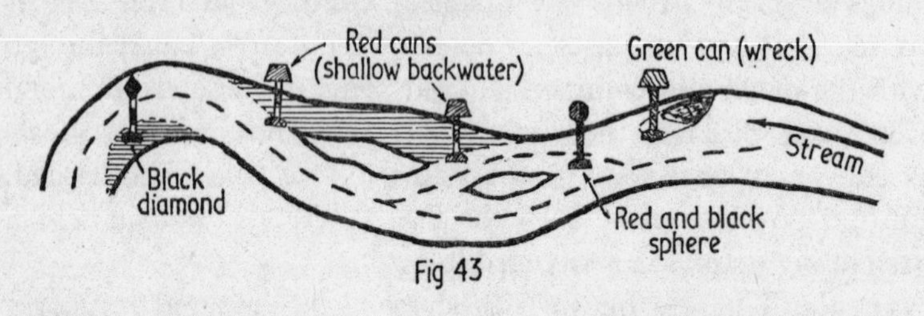

Fig 43

At bridges on tidal or commercial rivers, the navigation span is marked with one or two red lights in the middle, and any arch which is closed to navigation is marked with three red lights or discs in an inverted triangle or by a single red disc or ball of straw suspended in the arch.

Dredgers and other static working craft may have cables and anchors out some distance across the river, by which they manoeuvre. Pass them only on the side on which a white flag or shape is displayed, never on the side with a red flag or shape.

These should be replaced by lights at night, accompanied by a white riding light at the masthead to form a triangle. Red flags, shapes or lights to both sides show either that the cables block the river completely, or (on a tideway) simply that they must be given a wide berth. Other static craft may carry other distinguishing patterns, but as a general rule will *not* carry the red, green and white navigation lights described later unless under way. Give them all a wide berth.

Sound Signals

To make your intentions absolutely clear to other craft, use your horn if necessary to give navigation signals as follows:
ONE short blast—'I am altering course to starboard'.
TWO short blasts—'I am altering course to port'.
THREE short blasts—'My engine is working astern'.
This last could mean either that you are slowing down, stopping, or actually reversing. On hearing a signal from another craft, if possible it is courteous to alter course if necessary to allow it to perform its manoeuvre. Give a signal yourself if it would clarify the situation, particularly if you cannot accommodate the intentions of the other.

If you are either out of control or cannot manoeuvre much due to towing another boat, engine trouble, or a line round the propeller, use the signal:
FOUR short blasts—'I am unable to manoeuvre'.
On Continental waterways, this is also used for 'You are *not* clear to overtake me'.

Other signals of general use, particularly by commercial craft, are:
FOUR short blasts followed by ONE long blast—'I am going about to starboard'.
FOUR short blasts followed by TWO long blasts—'I am going about to port'.
FIVE or more short blasts—'I do not consider you are taking sufficient action to avoid me.'

This somewhat aggressive signal is rarely appropriate for use by small craft, and this applies also to the following:
ONE prolonged blast—'I am about to get under way' or 'I am claiming right of way over you' (eg at a bridge).
ONE long and ONE short blast—'I am about to overtake on your starboard side'.
ONE long and TWO short blasts—'I am about to overtake you on your port side'.
TWO long blasts—'I am stopping' (continent of Europe only).

If you take your boat on a coastal trip, be warned that local signals often have completely different meanings from those above, even at neighbouring ports in the same area.

Do not give nor rely on hand signals, which are easily misunderstood and not officially recognised. For example, a dinghy sailor holding out a hand to one side may be either indicating that he is turning that way, or inviting you past on that side. You *must* have a horn, and must know how to use it. On no account use it for any other purpose, or it may be misunderstood and cause an accident. It is not there for attracting the attention of someone on the bank, nor of lock keepers (who often take longer if hooted at), nor is there a signal for 'get out of my way'. There are plenty of appropriate signals to choose from, and if the other boat happens to be unpowered, he probably has right of way over you anyway.

Speed and Wash

Craft may not travel at high speeds on inland waterways in the British Isles, except when towing a skier on certain designated reaches. On most canals, the limit is 4mph, and in any case on a narrow or shallow waterway a greater speed is impossible for most craft because the propeller pushes water backwards, causing a heavy wash which can damage the banks and contribute to silting, not to mention the waste of fuel. Slightly higher speeds are permissible on most large rivers: 8mph is suggested on the upper Thames, 6mph on the Yorkshire Ouse (5mph through

York), 10mph on the lower Avon (but 4mph on the upper Avon). The maximum permissible speed of any boat is governed by the amount of wash it makes, and is usually much lower than these suggested limits. Look back at your wash frequently, and use it as your speedometer. Slow down when passing small craft which might be swamped, moored boats which might be thrown against bank or bottom and damaged, engineering works such as dredging, surveying and bank protection, and at any other time when a heavy wash might endanger or disturb others, banks or boats. An amplitude (ie the difference in height between the top of a wave and the bottom of a trough) of more than 6in might be considered excessive; a breaking wave at the bank certainly is.

If on the other hand you prefer to travel really slowly, which many consider to be the only way fully to appreciate the beauty of the waterways, give other craft an opportunity to overtake you if they wish.

Lights

When navigating between sunset and sunrise (which are *not* the lighting-up times for the road), you must show the proper navigation lights as in Fig 44. The masthead light should show through 225° ahead, stern light through 135° astern (so that one or other will be visible all round), and the port and starboard lights from dead ahead through 112½° to their own side only, so that the course

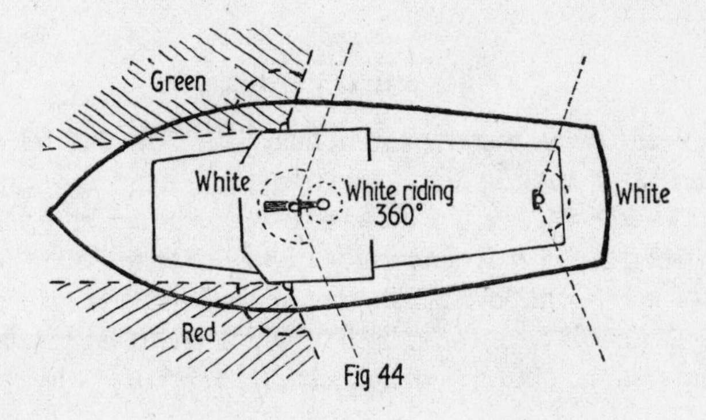

Fig 44

of another vessel can be estimated from the lights visible. If anchored or moored near the navigation channel or to a jetty marked with red lights (on a tideway), you do not need navigation lights provided you have a white riding light at the masthead, visible all round.

It is unwise not to have navigation lights fitted, for although you may have no intention of navigating after dark, delays can occur which make it unavoidable.

A spotlight must only be used for negotiating a tunnel or picking up a mooring. Do not drive along like a car using it as a headlight. This is illegal, because it does not comply with the system described above, and dazzles oncoming traffic and walkers on the towpath; and in any case you can see much better without it. It is never absolutely dark on the water, and although a headlight illuminates everything nearby within its beam, it effectively obliterates everything outside it. You need to see in *all* directions to navigate a boat.

Should you be out in an unpowered boat at night, including your tender, you are required to carry a torch or hurricane lantern that you can show in time to avoid a collision. A similar safeguard is essential on a powered boat caught out after dark, but although it may prevent an accident this would not satisfy any legal or practical requirements. The very fact that craft moving at night are rare means that those which do must take particular care to be properly and conspicuously lighted.

RIGHTS AND COURTESIES

Unlike road travel, a waterway holiday is a slow and leisurely thing, and it is not important whether the other fellow gets to the lock before you, or if you have to wait for him at a narrow bridge when really it is your right of way. Yet the question of rights of way is important, in that it forms the key to good manners and safe navigation, both of which are easier to achieve at leisure than in a hurry. Fortunately for everybody, while there are a few who will insist on *taking* right of way, most will readily *concede* it to others where due, and can reasonably expect others to do the same. In the event of an accident, such as a collision, it becomes fundamentally important to establish which craft had right of way, in any insurance claim or legal proceedings.

Rights of way on inland waterways are as much traditional as legal requirements, so it must be stressed that this chapter should not be taken as the ultimate authority on the matter, particularly in the event of any dispute. They do vary in some cases on different waterways. Craft proceeding with the stream (where there is any) normally have right of way over those going against it at narrow bends, bridges, etc, although a craft overtaking even with the stream does not have right of way over oncoming traffic.

Notwithstanding this, there is a custom that 'steam gives way to sail'. Dating from when manoeuvrable new steamers were replacing sailing ships, this has become extended to refer to all powered craft on one hand and all unpowered ones on the other, though it is wise to consider the relative size and manoeuvrability of the craft concerned. It would seem unreasonable as well as highly dangerous to row your dinghy downstream towards a bridge and insist on your right of way over the coaster punching up against the ebb!

The tradition does have relevance on the courses of rowing or sailing regattas. The former are normally well policed, and reasonable space left for launches to pass the course, but this space is also shared by crews making for the start. Sailing craft often have to tack to and fro across the river in order to use the wind. Slow down and go behind each boat—'under its stern'—unless you can pass by a different course without getting in its way. Naturally when there are about fifty of them all going in different directions, this may not be possible, though it is exciting to do so if your boat is small and handy. When meeting or overtaking sailing boats 'running before' the wind or otherwise keeping straight along the river instead of tacking, do so up-wind of them. Then, in the event of a sudden gust or mis-management of the sailing craft, it will tend to be blown away from you instead of across your course.

If it is not practicable to manoeuvre round sailing craft, just keep fairly well to the side and be prepared to slow down or speed up to avoid the odd one which comes a bit close, but it is surprising how well they can manage without using the one bit of water you are occupying. Sailing races are won and lost on skill, and good dinghy sailors will not let the presence of launches put them out of a race!

Canals

On a canal, you are not likely to meet sailing craft, though there are a good many kayaks, a few dinghies, and even the odd skiff and camping punt. In all cases, slow down so as not to swamp them or throw them against the bank.

Locks

The water in a canal is virtually static, and at locks and bridge holes the rule is 'first come, first served'. Should two boats arrive at a lock within sight of each other, the lock belongs to whichever it is ready for. If it is about half full due to leakage, the boat going *up* should have it, so that it will only have to be filled once then left empty. The golden rule is that you never draw a single sluice if this will waste a drop of water which another boat could have used.

Near a lock, particularly where there is a lock keeper's house, please be careful not to intrude on private gardens or other property. Just because a chap lives or works on a waterway, there is no reason why he should be subjected to people or dogs trampling over his garden, latecomers knocking on his door for assistance, and disturbance by shouting, playing radios, rattling lock gear unnecessarily (often late at night), and all the other antisocial things which a few people seem to think necessary for the enjoyment of their holiday.

Commercial Craft

It is a good principle (and the law in some areas) that commercial craft should take priority over pleasure craft, as they have a job to do, money to earn (often not much of it), and without them and their predecessors there would not *be* any navigable waterways in any case.

Overtaking

The onus is always on the overtaking boat to give way to the overtaken one, though most people if not in a hurry will usually pull to the side or even stop to allow a slightly faster boat to pass. If this courtesy is not extended, you have no right to demand it, and must only overtake if you can do so without interfering with the progress of the other boat or of oncoming craft. The correct side is normally to port of the other, but this will depend upon the circumstances. If you are the craft being overtaken, take care not to interfere with the other by altering course or increasing speed.

Should you happen to be behind a racing boat such as a sculler, an increase in speed to pass will probably sink him. With little effort, he can probably leave you standing anyway, and as they rarely go more than a few miles from the boathouse, he is unlikely to be in your way for long. Remain behind unless invited past, and remember that you cannot pass a small boat at close quarters without considerable disturbance to its progress.

Towing Paths

As the name implies, these were provided for the purpose of towing boats with horses or by hand, and anyone wishing to do so still has right of way over walkers, anglers, moored craft, and anything and everything else. If you meet a horse-drawn barge (and there are a few) pass it on the outside, ie away from the towpath.

In these days of scarce towed traffic, you can normally moor to the towpath provided you do not obstruct craft negotiating locks, bends or bridge holes. River towpaths often cross private property, and whereas towing is or was a right, mooring is entirely at the discretion of the owner. Therefore do not moor on fields without permission from the farmer, or on private gardens or land on the opposite side to the towpath. Most towpaths are also designated as public footpaths, and must not be obstructed by mooring lines, tents, picnics or fishing tackle. Be careful not to break away chunks by driving in mooring pegs too close to the edge.

Moorings for sanitary stations and lock lay-bys must only be used for their intended purposes, as many are used even 'after hours'.

Anglers

Most of our inland waterways are used more by anglers than by boats. Many pay licence fees, just as you do, and have just as much right to their hobby as you to yours. For your part, try to disturb them as little as possible with your wash, and keep in midstream to avoid floats and lines. Apart from being expensive for the angler to replace, fishing line round the propeller can immobilise you and cause expensive damage to shaft bearings and couplings.

POSTSCRIPT

I hope that this book has proved helpful to all who use the inland waterways for pleasure boating, or who are considering doing so, and that the vast majority of careful and courteous people will forgive the emphasis placed on points of courtesy and safety. Experience has shown that there is always a minority which finds it difficult to take such matters seriously, and I firmly believe that it is up to all of us to help such people understand and respect the ways of life afloat.

To all who have caught the boating bug, whether as a hobby which occupies all spare time or as an annual holiday, there is '. . . nothing which is quite so much fun as simply messing about in boats' (to quote Kenneth Grahame); and nothing as rewarding as doing so with skill and ease, without disturbing others or being disturbed by them, all enjoying your own kind of boating in your own way. That is what it is all about.

INDEX